Anonymous

Report of the Committee of the Overseers of Harvard College

Appointed to procure a perfect copy of the college charter, and to lay the same before the board, etc. With explanations and remarks respecting the construction of the third clause of said. Vol. 5

Anonymous

Report of the Committee of the Overseers of Harvard College
Appointed to procure a perfect copy of the college charter, and to lay the same before the board, etc. With explanations and remarks respecting the construction of the third clause of said. Vol. 5

ISBN/EAN: 9783337307936

Printed in Europe, USA, Canada, Australia, Japan

Cover: Foto ©ninafisch / pixelio.de

More available books at **www.hansebooks.com**

REPORT

OF THE

COMMITTEE OF THE OVERSEERS

OF

HARVARD COLLEGE,

APPOINTED TO PROCURE A PERFECT COPY OF THE

COLLEGE CHARTER,

AND TO LAY THE SAME BEFORE THE BOARD, ETC.

WITH EXPLANATIONS AND REMARKS RESPECTING THE CONSTRUCTION
OF THE THIRD CLAUSE OF SAID CHARTER.

SUBMITTED FEBRUARY 20, 1862.

BOSTON:
PRINTED BY GEO. C. RAND & AVERY,
No. 3 CORNHILL.
1862.

REPORT.

IN BOARD OF OVERSEERS OF HARVARD COLLEGE,
February 20, 1862.

THE Committee of the Overseers, appointed at the stated meeting of the Board, held at Cambridge on the 21st of June, 1860, to procure an accurate and perfect copy of the Charter of Harvard College, and to lay the same before this Board, and also to compare said copy with what purports to be a copy of said charter, as set forth in the first volume of the Records of the Overseers, and to ascertain what discrepancies and differences, if any, exist between them, and to make such explanations and remarks as they should consider pertinent, have attended to the duty assigned them, and present the following Report: —

In the year 1855, a committee of the Overseers was appointed to consider and report on the relative powers, duties and responsibilities of the Corporation and of the Overseers of Harvard College, which committee made a report on the 31st of January, 1856, and the same was accepted by this Board.

In said report it was in substance held and maintained by the said committee, that, from the four provisions of the third clause of the charter, the President and Fellows of Harvard College derived their power to make appointments, establish salaries, make removals of college officers, and to make orders and by-laws, and that the Overseers had the right of approval or disapproval of the orders or votes of the Corporation, by which such appointments, allowances, removals, and orders and by-laws were made, and that the Overseers had this right by virtue of the proviso to said third clause; said committee also maintained that the word *orders* in said proviso had the same meaning as the word *votes.*

A committee of conference was afterwards appointed by the President and Fellows to confer with a like committee of the Overseers, and to take into consideration, and report to said Corporation, the nature and extent of the rights and powers claimed by them, and of the corresponding duties and obligations of said Corporation. This committee of the President and Fellows made a report on the 15th of November, 1856, which was accepted by their Board. In said report to the President and Fellows, the committee admitted, in substance, that the powers of the Corporation, as to making appointments, allowances, removals, and orders and by-laws, were derived from the third clause of the charter, but they denied the right, claimed by the Overseers, of approval or disapproval of the votes of the Corporation in relation not only to salaries, but to appointments and removals, and insisted that such right of the Overseers, conferred upon them by the proviso to the third clause, was confined to the votes by which the Corporation were authorized to pass orders and by-laws by the fourth part or provision of said clause. Said committee of the Corporation also maintained that the word *orders* in said proviso did not signify *votes,* but meant the same as the words *orders and by-laws.*

The aforesaid report to the Overseers on the 31st of January, 1856, will hereinafter be referred to by your committee as the *report to the Overseers of January,* 1856, and the said report to the Corporation on the 15th of November, 1856, will be hereinafter referred to as the *report to the Corporation of November,* 1856.

The word *orders,* unconnected with the word laws, or the word by-laws, occurs in one instance only in the act of the General Court, found in the records of the Governor and Company of the Massachusetts Bay in New England, by which act, adopted at the session which commenced May 23, 1650, and commonly called the Charter, Harvard College was made a corporation; and a question has been raised, as aforesaid, respecting the meaning and force of the word *orders,* so standing alone.

For the purpose of determining this question, your Committee have examined with care the records of said Governor and Company, and the records of the colony of New Plymouth in New England. They have also examined the records of corporations, established prior to and since the Revolution of 1776, including therein those of the Corporation of Harvard College, and of towns, which are quasi corporations, in which records are set forth the doings of said corporations and towns, that occurred during our colonial and provincial history, and since the adoption of the Constitution of the Commonwealth of Massachusetts.

Like the African, East India, and other old English companies, the Governor and Company of the Massachusetts Bay in New England were incorporated for the purpose of carrying on trade, as well as establishing a plantation or colony, and in the outset held, like said companies, their meetings in London.

The charter of the said Governor and Company, which passed the seals March 4, 1628–9, in the fourth year of the reign of King Charles the First, provided that the freemen or members of the company should choose from their own number a Governor, Deputy Governor, and eighteen Assistants, who should hold monthly — or oftener, if they saw fit — a meeting, called the Court of Assistants, to take care for the best disposing and ordering of the general affairs of the colony, and the plantation thereof, and the government of the people there, and for handling, ordering and despatching of all such business and occurrents as should from time to time happen, touching or concerning the said company or plantation.

Four times a year a great and solemn assembly of the Governor, Deputy Governor, and such assistants and freemen as should choose to attend, was to be holden, called the Great and General Court of the Company (the Governor or Deputy Governor and seven Assistants being necessary to form a quorum), at which court they might choose other persons to be free of said company, — *constitute and appoint such officers as they should see fit and requisite for the ordering, managing and despatching of the affairs of said Governor and Company, and their successors,* and from time to time to make, ordain and establish all manner of wholesome and reasonable orders, ordinances, directions and instructions, laws and statutes, not contrary to the laws of England, for the welfare of the Company, and for the government of the plantation and the people inhabiting it; and for the imposition of lawful fines, mulcts, imprisonments, and other lawful corrections, according to the course of *other corporations* in the realm of England.

The said Company, having, before the date of the charter, purchased the territory over which it extends, from the Plymouth Company in England, had already, in 1628, sent out a number of settlers, who were planted in Salem. The great object of the colonists was to establish their own forms of church government and discipline, in a place where they might live unmolested. A number of substantial and respectable gentlemen were willing to settle permanently in the new plantation, provided the patent and government should be legally transferred, and be established, to remain with them and others inhabiting it.

The Company, on the motion of Matthew Cradock, the first Governor in England, agreed that it should be thus transferred; and in consequence of this arrangement, at a General Court, held at Mr. Goff's house, on Tuesday, the 20th of October, 1629, John Winthrop was chosen Governor for the ensuing year, to begin on the day last aforesaid. At the said meeting, prior to the said election, Governor Cradock caused to be read an *order*, formerly presented, concerning the buying of the ship Eagle, and desired to know the pleasure of the Court, for confirmation thereof. Whereupon, some debate being had, the *order* was approved of.

The meetings of the Governor and Company were held in England for a period of more than twelve months after the date of the charter, — all which meetings took place in London, except the last two, which were Courts of Assistants, one of which was held at Southampton, and the other, on the 23d of March, 1629-30, on board the Arbella, in Southampton harbor.

The next meeting, being a Court of Assistants, was held at Charlestown, August 23, 1630. Two other Courts of Assistants were held at Charlestown; afterwards the meetings were held in Boston, the first of which, being that of a General Court, took place on the 19th of October, 1630.

In the small beginnings of the colony all business, excepting the election of officers and the admission of freemen, appears to have been transacted indifferently in the General Court or in the Court of Assistants. But the people soon indicated that they were jealous of their liberties, and at an early period, when the acts and doings of these courts partook in any degree of the nature of rules and regulations, — that is, of laws, — the people insisted that such acts and doings should not take place in the Court of Assistants, but in the General Court only.

Prior to the time that the charter and government were transferred and removed to New England, the proceedings at the meetings of the Governor and Company related to the purchase or hiring of vessels, the fitting of the same for sea, the procuring of crews, provisions, clothing, arms, horses, cattle, fowls, books, seeds, and all such things as might be wanted by the passengers on the voyage, or after their arrival. So at the meetings in Charlestown, and at the early meetings in Boston, after Governor Winthrop and his company landed on these shores, the acts and doings of the courts related to all those small and necessary things which pertained to the first settlement in a wilderness.

When these courts were held in England, and for a considerable period afterwards, the proceedings were conducted with much simplicity. At the time John Winthrop was elected Governor in England, as above stated, he was chosen " by a general vote and full consent, by *the erection of hands.*"

The acts and doings of these courts were, for several

years, in many respects similar to those of common corporations, and during the whole colonial period, propositions and motions were not unfrequently made in the General Court, and phraseology was used, similar to what might occur in the transactions of an ordinary association, or mere business company.

The word *orders* was used to describe or denote the action of the General Court as well as that of the Court of Assistants, and their acts and doings were denominated orders. The word order signified the action of either of these bodies, by which they expressed their judgment, opinion, or will, or made their decision, whether the matter acted on was great or small, important or unimportant, of a general character, or related to some particular or individual case.

On almost all occasions the acts and doings of the General Court were introduced by the phrase, "*It is ordered.*" Thus we find in these records provisions of this sort, viz.: *It is ordered*, That a certain person be appointed captain, or agent, &c.; *ordered*, that his salary, or pay, be so many pounds; *ordered*, that a certain officer be removed. We find orders to pay Mr. Dunster, President of Harvard College, several sums of money, on account of his salary.

Whenever the action of the General Court is introduced by the words, "It is ordered," and a reference is afterwards made to such action in some subsequent proceedings of the General Court, such action is denominated an order. There is in the records of the General Court a considerable number of cases where the action of the court is introduced by the phrase "It is voted." In a small number of instances the phrase is, "It is resolved."

On examining the records of the General Court of the colony, as contained in five quarto volumes, published by virtue of two resolves of the Legislature of Massachusetts in the years 1853 and 1854, your Committee found the whole number of pages to be 2549. They then noted the instances wherein the action of the General Court is introduced by the phrase, or words, "It is ordered," on a certain large number of these pages. They next looked over, though less particularly, the residue of the 2549 pages aforesaid, and assuming that this phrase occurred in said residue as often, on an average, as in those pages in which the instances were carefully counted as aforesaid, your Committee came to the conclusion that the number of times in which the action of the court was introduced by the words "It is ordered," was 4253. Therefore there are in these volumes about 4253 orders.

In a large number of cases the action of the court relates to a class of matters of the same kind, and in these instances the action of the General Court is accomplished generally by an order, and sometimes by a vote. There are found in these records the phrases, "It is ordered and voted," and "It is voted and ordered;" "It is ordered and resolved;" "It is resolved and ordered;" "It is ordered and declared;" and *orders* are called *votes*, and *votes* are called *orders*. The General Court is sometimes adjourned by a *vote*, and sometimes it is adjourned by an *order*, showing conclusively that the word *order* has the same meaning and force as *vote*, and is used to accomplish precisely the same purpose.

Your Committee believe they have now demonstrated that the meaning of the word *orders*, when used in the proceedings of the colonial legislature, is substantially the same as that of *votes* or *resolutions*; such, certainly, was its original meaning. But after a time it acquired a secondary meaning. Although it retained its original sense in its full force, it acquired by degrees a secondary signification in this way: In the day of small things of the corporate body denominated the Governor and Company of the Massachusetts Bay in New England, the action of the Assistants, and also of the General Court, related to individual or separate matters. There was no generalization. Few, if any, rules had been adopted in conformity with which divers matters or classes of matters were to be regulated, settled or transacted. The consequence was, that special action was had in every case, and everything was disposed of without the aid of, or reference to, any general rule or regulation.

But about the time it was decided to remove the charter and government to New England, it became necessary to adopt certain *general* orders, which partook in some degree of the nature of rules and regulations, and afterwards, in the course of a few years, there were adopted by the General Court, at their sessions in Boston, divers further general orders of a more important character, which might well be denominated LAWS.

Throughout the colonial history, commencing about the third or fourth year after the arrival of Gov. Winthrop, the General Court appointed divers committees to peruse and examine all the acts and doings of the court of every kind or nature, general and special, passed from the beginning, or at a particular session (which acts and doings were almost universally accomplished by orders), and to select out from all the said acts and doings those orders which partook of the character of rules and regulations, or laws, and "to collect, collate, abbreviate, or enlarge, revise, digest, compile and prepare the same for publication."

Thus the particular orders by which rules, regulations and laws were adopted, began to be identified with the same, and so the word orders was at the first occasionally used to denote rules, regulations and laws. In this way it acquired a new or secondary signification.

There was no subject about which so much interest was manifested by the members of the General Court, and amongst the magistrates and people, as that which related to the laws. During a period of about half a century, the General Court in about a hundred instances appointed committees or took other action touching this matter; and the language used in their acts and doings on these occasions was laws, sometimes liberties, or liberties and laws, sometimes body of liberties, — then orders and statutes, then general orders, and laws and orders.

There evidently was a diversity of opinion as to the word or words which should be used to designate the laws, or any code or digest thereof. Zealous friends of liberty preferred one designation, and stern lawyers another.

It very soon was perceived that as the word *orders* could not, strictly speaking, be considered as an act of the court, but the means by which an act was adopted; and as the word had an original and well-established meaning, which was the same as that of votes, it was found convenient and necessary to connect this word, when used to indicate a rule or regulation, with laws or some kindred word. The phrase general orders was sometimes used at the first. But *laws and orders* were regarded as the most appropriate combination. In the remarks of the Hon. Francis C. Gray, on the early laws of Massachusetts, from which your Committee have made several extracts, is to be found the following passage: " The fact, that almost all the articles in the Body of Liberties are in substance contained in every subsequent Digest of the colony laws, shows that the people were not dissatisfied with its provisions. But they still desired a more minute and complete code, to include all the LAWS AND ORDERS of general observation."

When the word orders bears the same signification as that of laws, or a signification analogous thereto, it always, or certainly almost always, is used in connection with laws, under the phrase *laws and orders,* or some equivalent expression. If the question be asked why these words are both used, it may be answered that, when some legislator or lawyer was appointed to peruse and examine all the acts and doings of the General Court, from the beginning, or for any particular period or session, and to select out all such as were laws or statutes, or in any way partook of the nature of rules and regulations, such person, in proceeding to make such selection and revision, would of course find certain acts or doings about which he might have some doubts. He might hesitate to raise them to so much importance as would be indicated by the designation of them as laws, and yet he might perceive they had the semblance of rules and regulations or of laws. Therefore he might well conclude to call them *laws and orders,* which phrase would be sure to be applicable to whatever was contained in the selection made by him. This course is often taken in other similar cases. *Orders* and *by-laws* are used by corporations and towns, and these combinations become familiar phrases, and a person at all accustomed to them would be sure to repeat both words. He would not use one and omit the other, unless some good reason should exist for his doing so, such as that the single word used had a very different meaning, when standing alone, from what it had in connection with the other, and that the word, with such different meaning, was the appropriate one for that particular place.

In the records of some corporations in Massachusetts, their acts and doings are introduced by the phrase, "It is ordered," and in others by the phrase, "It is voted." Sometimes, in the same corporation or body, the phrase used is, "It is voted;" sometimes the phrase used is, "It is ordered." In the same way, it appears, by the records of some towns, which are quasi corporations, that their acts and doings are introduced by the phrase, "It is ordered," while in other towns the introductory phrase is, "It is voted;" and in the acts and doings of the same town the words "It is ordered" are sometimes used, and in others the phrase is "It is voted." But whatever may be the introductory phrase, the action of the town from time to time is generally designated by the word *orders*, while in some instances it is designated by the word *votes*. This was the course of things before the Revolution, and has been since.

Whenever the acts and doings of towns are rules and regulations, or partake of the nature thereof, they are called *orders and by-laws*. In the city of Boston, it appears by the records, that the acts and doings of the Mayor and Aldermen, and also of the Common Council, are introduced by the phrase, "It is ordered." All acts and doings are denominated orders, whether they relate to appointments, salaries, removals, or any matters other than rules and regulations, which are called *ordinances*, it having been especially provided by an express order of the City Council, that all acts in the nature of *orders and by-laws* should be styled *ordinances*.

Under the colonial government, whenever a corporation was established, such corporation was authorized to make "orders and by-laws," and similar authority was possessed by the towns; and since the Revolution all towns have been, and now are, by the laws of the Commonwealth, expressly empowered to adopt "orders and by-laws."

It appears by the records of the Plymouth Colony, that the acts and doings of the Court of Assistants, and of the General Court, were generally introduced by the phrase, "It is ordered," and the results of the action of the Court were denominated orders, or rather *court orders*. They were called *court* orders, because they were adopted by a body called a *court*.

From the foregoing history, it appears that whenever the word orders, standing alone, was used in any statute or act of incorporation of the General Court, or in any act of a corporation or town, the meaning was the same as votes or resolutions. Such was its primary and original meaning; and when it was used in its secondary signification, denoting rules and regulations, this was indicated by its connection with the word *laws*, constituting the phrase "laws and orders," or *orders and by-laws*.

Although, as it has been stated, the judgment, opinion, will or decision of the General Court of the colony were sometimes expressed by *votes* or *resolutions*; yet, as these words were comparatively quite rarely used, and when used, they had the same signification as the word *orders*, and as the word *orders*, in a very great majority of cases, expressed and described the action of the court, it became the *prevailing* word to denote such action whenever the proceedings of the court during a particular session, or the whole period after the arrival of Gov. Winthrop, were spoken of, or mentioned.

Your Committee will here introduce an incident that occurred during the administration of Gov. Shute, which goes to demonstrate that during our colonial history the words orders, votes or resolutions, though one of them might occasionally be used as in some slight degree more applicable, according to the nature of the subject, to this or that case, than either of the other words, were all three generally used to express the same meaning.

In the year 1722, the House of Representatives, upon the memorial of the Overseers of Harvard College, adopted certain "resolutions," which were concurred in by the Council, and presented to Gov. Shute for his assent. These "resolutions" the Governor returned, with a conditional approval only, as follows, viz.: " I consent to these *votes*, provided the Rev. Mr. Benjamin Wadsworth, and the Rev. Mr. Benjamin Colman, and the Rev. Mr. Appleton, are not removed by said *orders*, but still remain Fellows of the Corporation." Here the words " resolutions," " votes," and " orders," were used to denote the same thing.

It is stated by the Hon. Josiah Quincy, in his able and elaborate History of Harvard University, " that the Proceedings of the President and Fellows of the college are recorded as being done ' at a meeting of the Corporation,' or introduced by the formula, ' It is ORDERED by the Corporation;'" and by the early records of the college prior to the date of the charter, at meetings of what were denominated "the governors of the college," it appears that when elections of officers and servants took place, and allowances or compensation were made to them, or any similar matter was transacted, the acts and doings were introduced by the phrase, "It is ORDERED."

Your Committee have examined also the records of the Corporation, containing their acts and doings for the period of half a century immediately succeeding the date of the charter, and they find the proceedings of that body, during these fifty years, were in most cases introduced by the formula, "It is *ordered*," and occasionally by the phrase, "It is voted;" and when the action of the Corporation, introduced by the phrase or formula, "It is ordered," is subsequently described or referred to, it is sometimes denominated an ORDER, and sometimes a VOTE, showing conclusively that the word ORDER was considered as having the same meaning as that of VOTE.

The action of the Corporation was therefore accomplished by *orders*, signifying the same as *votes*, in perfect accordance with what the framer of the third clause of the charter intended and contemplated by the language used by him, when he drew the same and composed the proviso to that clause.

Your Committee have caused to be inserted in an Appendix several extracts from the early records of the college, showing in what form and by what means the action of the "Governors of Harvard College," prior to the 31st of May, 1650, and of the "Corporation" afterwards, was effected, and they ask the particular attention of the friends of the college to the record of these proceedings.

If the language of our statesmen, legislators and scholars, — especially of those most familiar with the legislation of the colonial and provincial periods, — is particularly noticed and scanned, it will be found, whenever an occasion arises for the use of the words orders, votes and resolutions, that these words, especially orders and votes, are used, or referred to, as equivalent or very similar expressions. Your Committee will not enlarge their report by referring to the writings of more than one of these statesmen, legislators and scholars, and they will cite from the writings of that one, whose thorough and accurate knowledge of the meaning and force of words is recognized everywhere.

The distinguished gentleman alluded to was educated at Harvard College, and has been a Tutor, Professor and President of the same. He has had experience as a legislator in the Senate and House of Representatives of the United States, and in the Cabinet at Washington as Secretary of State. He also has been Governor of Massachusetts, and of course presided at the Council Board, whose acts and doings are introduced by the phrase "It is ordered," and are denominated *orders*.

Your Committee presume it is already understood to whom reference is made, and they will now proceed to cite two or three instances, out of many which may be found, to prove that the Hon. Edward Everett uses the words *orders* and *votes* as equivalent expressions.

In the preface to a new edition of the laws concerning Harvard University, written by Mr. Everett, when President of the college, and bearing date Nov. 16, 1848, he uses the following language, viz.: "At length, on the 12th of Sept., 1846, the President was requested, by a *vote* of the Corporation, 'to consider and ascertain the present state of the college laws, and to make report.' This *vote* of the Corporation was understood to contemplate a complete revision of the statutes and laws of the University.

" In pursuance of this *order*, on the 27th of November of the last year, a revised code of laws was reported by the President to the Corporation, and by them ordered to be privately printed, with a view to its consideration by the two Boards. At the following meeting, on the 27th of December, it was laid before the Corporation in a printed form. It was *ordered* by the Corporation at the same time, that a printed copy should be furnished to each member of the college Faculty, and to the Faculty of each professional school, with the request that they should submit to the Corporation in writing such remarks as they might think proper to make on any part of the proposed code.

" On the 15th of January of the present year the revised code, as reported by the President, was, in connection with the remarks of the members of the Faculties, taken up for consideration by the Corporation, at a special meeting called for this purpose, and it was further considered at several adjourned meetings in the course of the winter and spring of 1848. Sundry amendments were adopted by the Corporation; and on the 23d of May, 1848, the revised code was ordered to be printed, as amended at that and the preceding meetings of the Board. Farther amendments were adopted at the meeting of the Corporation on the 27th of May, and on the 10th of June last the following ORDERS were passed: —

" *Voted*, That the Revised Laws of the college, as submitted at the last meeting, be adopted by the Board, and it was ordered that the same be signed and certified by the Secretary.

" *Voted*, That the President be requested to lay the laws, as adopted, before the Board of Overseers, that they may concur in the same, if they see fit."

Your Committee come now to the consideration of that part, before referred to herein, of the charter of Harvard College, granted by the General Court, and bearing date May 31st, 1650. This part of the charter is commonly denominated the *third* clause thereof, and is as follows, viz. : " And the President and Fellows, or the major part of them, from time to time, may meet and choose such officers and servants for the college, and make such allowance to them, and them also to remove, and, after death or removal, to choose such others, and to make from time to time such orders and by-laws, for the better ordering and carrying on the work of the college, as they shall think fit; *provided* the said ORDERS be allowed by the Overseers."

This clause is a very important part of the charter, and confers several large powers. The clause may be divided into four parts, or provisions ; — the *first* giving the power to the President and Fellows to choose officers and servants; the *second*, to make allowance to them — that is, to prescribe their salaries ; the *third*, to remove them ; and the *fourth*, to make orders and by-laws.

The President and Fellows, by accepting the report aforesaid of their committee of November, 1856, have substantially declared that their power to elect and appoint instructors, officers and servants of the college, is derived from, and rests upon, this third clause, and that they possess, by virtue of said clause, the power to make allowances to such instructors and officers, and to make removals and orders and by-laws. There is not, therefore, any difference of opinion on this subject between the two Boards; certainly none so far as the appointments, the salaries and removals of *officers of instruction and government are concerned.*

The question then arises whether the Overseers have, by virtue of the proviso to said third clause, the right of concurrence or non-concurrence in relation to the exercise of the powers in the third clause of the charter, conferred upon the President and Fellows.

For the first time in the history of the college, it was distinctly asserted on behalf of the Corporation, in the report of Nov., 1856, to that Board, that the said proviso, in the following words, " Provided the said *orders* be allowed by the Overseers," applied to the fourth provision only of said third clause, by which provision the President and Fellows are authorized " from time to time to make orders and by-laws for the better ordering and carrying on the work of the college;" and it is in fact insisted in said report that the Overseers have no right of approval or disapproval of the votes of the Corporation by which they elect officers of instruction and government.

As to this doctrine set up on the part of the Corporation, your Committee make answer: In *the first* place, the words, " as they shall think fit," at the conclusion of all the substantive enactments in said third clause, apply to each of said four provisions. Of this there can be no possible question, and the presumption therefore is, that the proviso immediately following the said words, " as they shall think fit," has as extensive an application as said concluding words of all said substantive enactments.

In *the second* place, your Committee insist with the utmost confidence that if the said proviso had been intended to apply to the said part or provision only, which relates to the making of *orders* and *by-laws*, it would have read as follows: provided the said *orders* and *by-laws* be allowed by the Overseers.

It is believed that not an instance can be found in the whole history of legislation in Massachusetts since Governor Winthrop came over with the colonial charter, down to the present time, where two important words, such as rules and regulations, or orders and laws, or orders and by-laws, have ever been used in a substantive enactment, which is followed by a proviso for the special purpose of qualifying said two words, and then in such proviso one of such words only is used, and the other is omitted. It is believed that no such thing ever occurred in the Legislature, or in the doings of any town, municipal or other corporation. It is a mistake not likely to occur. Indeed, it may be pronounced the most unlikely thing that could happen. Members of the General Court, selectmen of towns, or directors of an ordinary corporation, may spell incorrectly, or commit many mistakes or blunders, but when, in drafting an act or vote, they use two important words, especially such as constitute a common and familiar phrase, which ought by all means to be repeated in a proviso, if a proviso is to be introduced for the purpose of so qualifying them, then such members, selectmen, or directors can hardly fail to repeat both words in such proviso.

If the chairman of a committee, or other person, had undertaken so important a work as to draft a college charter, and he had inserted the words orders and bylaws in a substantive enactment, as in this case, and then the next instant he had proceeded to compose a very short proviso, containing a single line, for the purpose of qualifying said substantive enactment,— that is, the most prominent part thereof,— is it possible that he would omit half of a familiar phrase, and leave out one of two words of special importance? Besides, had the bill been so drawn, with the word *by-laws* omitted in the proviso, and the obvious design and intention of the bill had been that it should be inserted, would not the committee on bills in the third reading, or the committee on engrossed bills, have detected the omission, and seized the opportunity to magnify their official consequence by correcting the error?

These circumstances go to prove conclusively that the word orders alone was manifestly the correct expression, and was used in the proviso by the person who drafted the charter, with *special intention,* so that a word, signifying the same as *votes,* should constitute the substantial part of the proviso, and make it applicable to not only the orders or votes by which orders and bylaws should be adopted, but to the orders or votes by which elections, allowances and removals should be made by virtue of the three first parts or provisions of the third clause.

In *the third* place, it should be borne in mind that the charter of Harvard College created the first corporation which was established by the colonial legislature, and no other corporation existed in the colony for some time afterwards. This charter deprived the General Court of divers powers they had previously possessed and exercised. It is somewhat remarkable that the friends of the college were able to obtain a charter, conferring such important powers as this did, subject even to the sanction or revision of the Overseers. Would it then have been possible to repress the jealousy which would have arisen against granting to a body, consisting of seven persons only, such important powers as are given to the Corporation by the third clause of the charter, *without* conferring on the Overseers the right of approval or disapproval?

It would have been very strange if the General Court had given to the Corporation full and uncontrolled authority to appoint all officers of instruction and government, to establish their salaries, and, above all, to make removals of any such officers, without the sanction of the Overseers, while the said court would not allow the same body, without the consent of the Overseers, to make any *orders* and *by-laws*, even such as related to the dress of the students at commencement, or on any other occasion, — or such as prohibited any student from ordering sizings at commons beyond the amount of forty shillings during one college term, or from being present at a class meeting without special license, — or from going to any tavern in Cambridge for the purpose of eating or drinking, — or keeping, without leave, any gun or pistol, horse, dog, or other animal (including, of course, a cat or a canary bird), in Cambridge. It certainly would have been quite extraordinary if the General Court of the colony had given to the Corporation full power to appoint a PROFESSOR OF DIVINITY, or of MATHEMATICS, and to establish their salaries, and to REMOVE them from office, without being obliged to consult the Overseers, or ask their approval; and yet that the court should have made it necessary to call together the Overseers, consisting of the Governor, Deputy Governor, and all the magistrates of the jurisdiction, with the teaching elders of the six adjoining towns, and require them to assemble for the purpose of giving validity to one or more petty orders and by-laws, adopted by the Corporation.

Fourthly. The President and Fellows have, in a formal manner, by accepting said report to them of Nov., 1856, admitted and declared, that " appointments, made by the Corporation, of officers of instruction and government, have from the earliest times, and, as is believed, with entire uniformity, been sent up to the Overseers for concurrence or rejection ; and that the submission to the Overseers of all appointments to offices of instruction and government has not only the sanction of antiquity coeval with the chartered existence of the college, but is of great moment as a safeguard against appointments from interested and private motives; and invests the officers thus confirmed with a sense of public responsibility, and with dignity and authority of great value in establishing effective influence over the scholars, and in elevating the character of the institution."

Can it be imagined that the General Court, in 1650, would have granted a charter with a defect so palpable as would have existed if the right of approval or disapproval of such appointments had not been conferred on the Overseers ?

In the year 1851 the President and Fellows presented a memorial to the House of Representatives, which was signed by the members of the Board. In this memorial they found it necessary to allude to the powers of the Corporation. They stated that " in Williams College, and in nearly all the colleges of the country, there is but one Board, consisting of members who hold perpetual succession, fill up their own vacancies, *make all appointments*, and transact the important business, without the control or advice of any other authority, and that in the exercise of power the Corporation is under much heavier restraints than is customary in other similar institutions." Again, in page 47 of said memorial, the Corporation say: " It " (the charter) " gave to them " (the Corporation) " the sole power of appointing all *officers* and *servants of the college,* and vested in them the exclusive right of enacting rules and laws for its government, and administering them, *subject only to the approval* or *disapproval* of *such appointments, rules and laws, by the Overseers.*"

Thus the Corporation in said memorial most distinctly and fully admit that the Overseers have the right of approval or disapproval of all votes by which the Corporation make orders and by-laws. Of course they refer to the proviso at the end of the third clause of the charter, by which the Overseers have, by universal admission, this right of approval or disapproval as to orders and by-laws; and the Corporation say in the very same connection, that the Overseers have this right as to appointments, and therefore they must have it by virtue of said proviso.

Again, it is expressly admitted and declared in the said report to the Corporation of Nov., 1856, that if said proviso applies to *appointments* it applies to *salaries;* consequently the Corporation by their memorial to the Legislature in 1851, and by the report of Nov., 1856, accepted by them, may well be considered as *having declared* that the Overseers have the right of approval or disapproval of the votes of the Corporation by which *appointments* are made and *salaries* are established.

Fifthly. Your Committee now come to the application of the evidence in relation to the meaning of the word *orders*, standing alone, which they have presented in the former part of their report, having derived the same from the records of the General Court of the colony and other bodies, and from the records of the Corporation of Harvard College; and they make the point that the word *orders*, so used in the proviso at the close of the third clause of the college charter, unconnected with the word by-laws, or other word or words of similar signification, must mean *votes* or *resolutions;* that is, the votes by which the President and Fellows make elections of "officers and servants of the college," also allowances and removals, and pass orders and by-laws, in conformity with the authority given to them in the four parts or provisions of said third clause.

There is no evidence or glimmering of evidence in said third clause, or in any other part of the charter, or in the appendix, tending to show that the word orders, standing alone in said proviso, signifies rules and regulations, or orders and by-laws, but the reasons before stated, and every circumstance connected with said clause, and other parts of the charter, or with the appendix, go to prove that the single word *orders* in this place must mean *votes.*

The phrase orders and by-laws occurs twice in the charter and three times in the appendix, whereas the word orders, standing alone, is found once only, and that is in the charter. In the first clause of the appendix there is a provision touching orders and by-laws, and that phrase is used in the substantive enactment, and then comes a proviso qualifying said principal or substantive enactment, and the same phrase, that is, both said words, *orders* and *by-laws*, is repeated. This may well be regarded as a very significant circumstance.

By considering the word orders in the proviso to the third clause of the charter as meaning *votes*, which is the universal signification thereof, when standing alone, or certainly almost the universal signification, everything is made plain, and every difficulty is removed. The whole of the third clause, and every part of it, thus becomes sensible, consistent, intelligible, reasonable, and free from all ambiguity and absurdity.

Your Committee will now set forth this third clause, with a substitution of the word *votes* for orders, and thus enable every one to perceive how simple and plain the whole clause appears, as follows, viz.: —

" And the President and Fellows, or the major part of them, from time to time, may meet and choose such officers and servants for the college, and make such allowance to them, and them also to remove, and, after death or removal, to choose such others, and to make from time to time such orders and by-laws, for the better ordering and carrying on the work of the college, as they shall think fit; *provided* the said *votes* be allowed by the Overseers."

Suppose the last provision in the third clause, by which authority is given to the Corporation to make orders and by-laws, had been wholly omitted, or had been inserted in some other part of the charter, entirely separate and distinct from the third clause, then the third clause would have read as follows, viz.: " And the President and Fellows, or the major part of them, from time to time, may meet and choose such officers and servants for the college, and make such allowance to them, and them also to remove, and, after death or removal, to choose such others, as they shall think fit; *provided* the said orders be allowed by the Overseers."

Would not such a clause have been perfectly plain and intelligible? and would there in such case have been any doubt whatever of the meaning of said proviso? Surely, the mere addition or insertion of the fourth part or provision as to the making of orders and by-laws, as it now stands in the third clause in the charter, cannot change the meaning of the other three parts or provisions, or the force and effect of the proviso, or affect its relation to said three first parts or provisions of the third clause.

It is quite certain that the person who drafted the charter, must, when he drew the third clause, constantly have had in his mind the fact that the Corporation would appoint officers and servants of the college, and remove them, make allowances to them, and pass orders and by-laws, in accordance with the practice in the General Court in similar cases. Therefore he, without doubt, regarded the four provisions of said clause as having the same meaning and effect as they would have had if the Corporation had been expressly authorized, by *orders* or *votes*, to make such appointments, allowances, removals, and orders and by-laws. Consequently, when he composed the proviso to said clause, he had special reference to said *orders* or *votes*, which he considered just as certainly implied and embraced in said provisions of said clause, as if the word *orders* or *votes* had been actually inserted therein. The words, " the said orders," therefore, in said proviso, so far from being of " doubtful interpretation," are the most apt and appropriate that could have been used " to convey a clear and certain allusion" to the making of appointments, allowances and removals, as well as to the passing of orders and by-laws.

The framer of said third clause well understood what was intended by said four parts or provisions thereof, and what would be the action of the Corporation by virtue of said provisions, and by what means their action would be accomplished. When, therefore, he proceeded to draw the proviso, which was to qualify such action, or the means by which it would be effected, he selected such fitting expression as should describe such action or means, and consequently used the phrase, "the said orders."

Although the language of the substantive enactments in said third clause is elliptical, and the means by which appointments, allowances, &c., are to be made by the Corporation are not expressly set forth, yet they are so plainly indicated that the same cannot be misunderstood, and the framer of said clause in composing a proviso, or subsequent condition thereto, did not hesitate, well understanding what the intention of said enactments was, to adopt a direct and specific term to describe such intention, and to express the means by which the Corporation was authorized to make appointments, allowances, removals, and orders and by-laws, and which were to be qualified by said proviso.

Of the committee of the Overseers, whose report, as hereinbefore stated, was made to that Board in January, 1856, the late Hon. Samuel Hoar was a member. Mr. Hoar was a warm friend of the several members of the Corporation, and entertained great respect for them. He at all times took a deep interest in the affairs, success and prosperity of the college, and was one of its most devoted and sincere friends. He had carefully studied the charter and the laws supplementary thereto. He was an able lawyer, and was particularly familiar with the statutes of the Commonwealth, and had carefully studied the legislation that arose during the colonial and provincial periods. He was in large and full practice at the bar for a period approaching half a century. He was a member of our State Senate and of our House of Representatives, and was a representative in the Congress of the United States. He was often present at ecclesiastical councils — sometimes as a delegate, and at other times as legal adviser and counsel. He had extensive knowledge of the affairs and doings of towns and corporations in Massachusetts, and was familiar with the language and phraseology used in their transactions and records.

At the first meeting of said committee of the Overseers, one of the members called the attention of Mr. Hoar to the second clause of the appendix to the college charter, and suggested that by the provisions of that clause the Overseers might be considered as possessing the right of revision as to all the acts and doings of the Corporation, without any exception. This suggestion did not meet with favor from Mr. Hoar, and he remarked that he was wholly opposed to the opening of an additional source of discussion, or to the raising of any question, predicated on this middle clause of the appendix, which might embarrass the Corporation, or lead to the setting up of a new construction adverse to the rights of that body. He said the Corporation had for more than two centuries been the bulwark of the college, and that he should be sorry to have a foundation laid for an attempt to impair or affect in any way the powers conferred upon them by the charter. He then observed that the committee had better confine their attention to the third clause of the charter, which gave to the Overseers all the control over the acts of the Corporation which they could desire. This clause, he said, expressly conferred divers important powers on the President and Fellows of the college, and by it they were authorized to make appointments, allowances, and removals, and to adopt orders and by-laws, the exercise of all which powers were made subject to the approval or disapproval of the Overseers, by the proviso at the end of said clause. He further remarked that his attention had been called to this part of the charter many years ago, and that the opinion he then formed and still entertained was, that the word orders in said proviso had the same meaning as that of votes, being the votes by which the Corporation should make appointments, &c.

The committee adopted the advice of Mr. Hoar, and concluded to regard the provisions of the third clause as containing the authority of the Corporation to make appointments, allowances, removals and orders and by-laws, and to consider the said proviso as giving to the Overseers the right of approval or disapproval of the orders or votes of the Corporation, by which they should make all such appointments, &c.

As the said committee of the Overseers could not find that there ever had been any discussion between the two Boards in relation to the special meaning and force of the word orders in said proviso, a suggestion was made that the committee should not go into an exposition of the position taken by them, and of the grounds of their opinion on this particular point, trusting that the Corporation would concur in the position so taken; but if the Corporation should dissent from the conclusions of said committee of the Overseers, and should express their views on the subject, then some future committee of the Overseers might make a full explanation and exposition as to the meaning of the word orders in said proviso; and the committee of this Board made their report in January, 1856, in accordance with said suggestion.

Your Committee will now ask the attention of the Overseers to the course of measures and doings of these Boards since the date of the charter, having a tendency to throw light upon the construction of that instrument, especially of the first part or provision of the third clause of the charter.

The Corporation has from the beginning employed, either directly or through the agency of others, suitable persons to render inferior and humble service, such as laborers, sweepers, carpenters, painters, glaziers, cook, butler, baker, brewer, master of the kitchen, and purveyor of commons, being all the ministerial agents or servants from the lowest up to that of steward, who at the beginning had charge of providing for the board of six or eight students, and possibly of two or three instructors or officers of government. The steward was master of the kitchen, and sometimes probably acted as chief cook, until, by the increase of the number of students, it became necessary to have an under steward, who took the special management of the affairs in the kitchen. The definition of "a steward in a college is the person who provides provisions for the students." This course has been at all times pursued by the Corporation without asking the formal approval of the Overseers. The question now arises, What was the origin of this practice, and may be considered as the legal effect thereof?

Upon the organization of the Corporation under the charter, there can be no doubt that the President and Fellows at once made a careful survey and examination of its provisions, and considered what construction thereof would be the true construction, and would be most beneficial to the interests of the institution, as well as most expedient on the whole for their own body, and most convenient and satisfactory to both Boards.

They well understood that the first great object of the charter was to establish a corporation, in which would be vested the title to all the property, real and personal, belonging to the college, and to give to said corporation the sole and absolute control and management of the same.

They at once perceived that, in order to secure this sole and absolute management of said property, it was expedient and requisite that the Corporation should employ and appoint all the agents and servants, through whom they could possess and retain this management. They must have seen the desirableness of their employing and appointing these agents and servants by virtue of an inherent and necessary power, which they might consider themselves as deriving from that primary and all-important enactment of the charter, by which said title was vested in, and said sole and exclusive management was virtually conferred upon, them. They undoubtedly preferred to exercise this power as an original and essential right, irrespective of the subsequent provisions of the charter, contained in the third clause, where there was a certain right of approval given to the Overseers, the construction of which might be a source of inconvenience to the Corporation.

With these views probably the President and Fellows chose and employed all the agents and servants of the college, from the steward inclusive down to the mere laborers, without asking the approval of the other Board; and they found no difficulty in pursuing this course, because the Overseers perceived it was, and would at all times be, *necessary*, and would be much more convenient to their Board, and more beneficial to the college than any other course.

The Overseers probably never knew or suspected that the Corporation might be influenced at the beginning by any such consideration as above suggested, with reference to an original, inherent and exclusive power on their part, in the employment or choice of the agents and servants aforesaid, without asking the approval of the Overseers. The Overseers, without doubt, verily supposed that the Corporation had adopted this course from a consideration of the intrinsic propriety and actual necessity of the thing, and with reference to the convenience of both Boards, and the Overseers for the same reasons acquiesced therein.

It is manifestly of no consequence whether the course, pursued as aforesaid in relation to this subject, had its origin in the desire and intention of the President and Fellows to keep in their own hands the sole and exclusive management of all the property belonging to the college by virtue of the inherent and incidental power aforesaid, or whether the President and Fellows considered themselves as choosing and employing the steward and the servants below him, by virtue of the third clause of the charter, and found it a matter of indispensable propriety and necessity to do this without the ceremony of laying a formal vote in every case before the Overseers for their approval or disapproval, and the Overseers assented at the beginning and ever afterwards to this course, with the same wise forecast and in the same good spirit with which the Corporation *appeared* to have adopted it. The practical effect was the same in either case.

Suppose the Overseers had, by virtue of what they considered their just rights, insisted that the Corporation should, at regular meetings, in a formal manner, by orders or votes, make appointments of laborers, perhaps such as might be employed to do some small job, and lay such orders or votes before the Overseers for their approval, and the members of the latter Board, consisting of the Governor, Deputy Governor, and thirty or forty other honorable and reverend gentlemen, had been called together to act upon such a matter, would not this, besides being excessively troublesome, have been regarded as quite ridiculous? The Overseers must have seen the importance and the manifest *necessity* of leaving all such matters, occurring every day, and perhaps several times a day (being, too, of a mere business character, and relating to the management of lands, buildings, and chattels), in the sole and exclusive charge of a small Board like that of the Corporation.

It was proper that there should be some understanding as to the limit to which this practice should extend, and there was an obvious propriety, when the charter went into operation, of beginning with the humblest servant, and extending the above practice as far as the steward — that is, to all below the grade or rank of officers of instruction and government. The students were required to take off their hats in the presence of the professors, tutors and other officers of instruction and government, and to exhibit some token of recognition and respect when passing them; but not so with regard to the steward and all servants below him. The steward, although an important functionary and standing in a place higher than that of some other individuals in the employment of the college, must at an early period have occupied a humble position. In Judge Sewall's diary is the following entry, under date of July 15, 1687: — "Andrew Boardman, steward and cook of Harvard College, buried."

For the first forty years the number of graduates was on an average about six annually, and for the first seventy-one years the average annual number was about nine. It certainly could not be a place of much dignity or consideration to provide food for six or nine boys, some of whom were, perhaps, young Indians, the education of whom was one of the expressed objects of the founders of the institution.

So also, at the beginning, the number of books which were the property of the college was small, and there does not appear to have been any regular librarian for the first seventeen years after the granting of the charter, and when, in 1667, a librarian was employed or appointed, the position must have been regarded as a humble one, and the same course was taken as to him as was pursued with regard to the inferior servants aforesaid, till the year 1767. When the librarian was first appointed, his rank was similar to that of the steward, and it was understood that the Corporation did not deem the employment or appointment of a librarian of sufficient importance to warrant the formality of consulting the other Board, or asking their consent or concurrence. The Overseers took the same view of the matter, and acquiesced very cheerfully in the course pursued by the Corporation till the year 1766, when, on the 6th of May, a committee of the Overseers, of which Lieut. Gov. Hutchinson was chairman, was appointed "to enquire into the state of the college, and to consider of such things as may be beneficial to it." This committee made a report, the conclusion of which was as follows: — "The committee are further of opinion that it would tend to strengthen and assist the government of the college if the librarian were vested with all the powers of tutors, and joined with them in the government of the society."

In pursuance of this suggestion of the Overseers, as it is presumed, the Corporation, at a meeting held soon afterwards, passed the following rule and regulation, viz. : —

"The librarian shall be appointed by the Corporation, with the consent of *the Overseers*, and shall have the like power and authority to punish the under-graduates for any disorders, or breaches of the college laws, as the tutors have; and he shall act in conjunction with the President and tutors in the government of the society in all their meetings; and with the President, professors, and tutors, in all such cases as come under their cognizance, and *shall be entitled to the same tokens of respect from the under-graduates as the tutors are;* and shall have a chamber assigned him by the Corporation, suitable for the inspection of some district in the college."

This act of the Corporation, having been laid before

the Overseers, was assented to by them. When your Committee, in their report, shall hereafter speak of the officers of instruction and government, they wish to have it understood that they consider the librarian as one of that number. The librarian, having thus been raised above the grade of the inferior servants aforesaid, and elevated to the rank of officer of instruction and government, the order or vote by which any person was afterwards appointed by the Corporation to fill that place was laid before the Overseers for their approval.

A formal declaration respecting the appointment of the librarian, and the right of approval or disapproval, on the part of the Overseers, of the action of the Corporation by which that officer is so appointed, was made by both Boards in the 138th article of the edition of 1848 of the laws concerning the university, which article is as follows, viz. : —

" The librarian is chosen, like the OTHER OFFICERS OF THE UNIVERSITY, by the Corporation, with the CONCURRENCE OF THE OVERSEERS; he is to continue in office during THEIR pleasure, and he shall be subject to removal for neglect of duty or misbehavior." Thus it appears that when the librarian was raised to the rank of an officer of government and instruction in the university, he stood on the same footing with those officers, as to his appointment and liability to be removed, the Overseers having the right of approval or disapproval in each case; and the marked distinction between such officers and the steward, as well as all the agents or servants below him, was continually kept up, and all matters relating to the steward and other inferior servants remained, without any questions being raised, in the same state as at the beginning, and subsequent thereto, till the year 1778.

During that year a vacancy occurred in the situation of steward, and the Corporation selected and employed Mr. William Kneeland to fill the same, in accordance with the previous practice, and the understanding of both Boards, that the Overseers should not be consulted, or take any part in relation to the matter. But it so happened that Mr. Kneeland being considered as unfriendly to the cause of American independence, the selection and employment of him by the Corporation to be steward was objectionable to some of the zealous whigs in the Board of Overseers. On this account it seems to have been thought expedient, in order that the Overseers might control the matter, to insist on their right to approve or disapprove the election of steward by the Corporation in all cases.

Accordingly, at a meeting of the Overseers in Dec., 1778, the following vote was passed, viz.: — "It being a matter in dispute between the Corporation and Overseers, whether the election of a college steward ought to be presented to this Board for their approbation, and the Board, not being in possession of the charters by which this point ought to be decided, it was voted that the *secretary* be directed to deliver to the president of the council, as soon as may be, *copies* of the charter granted by the General Court in the year 1642, and of that granted in 1650, and of the appendix, granted in 1657, for the inspection of the Overseers, that they may the better be able to discuss the matter in dispute, and come to a determination upon it at the adjournment of this meeting."

On the 16th of said December this adjourned meeting took place, twenty-three members being present; and the record states, that "after some debate it was moved that the question should be put, whether this Board have a right to a presentation of the person, elected by the Corporation in the office of steward, for their approbation or disapprobation; whereupon the *previous* question was moved, whether this question shall be now put, — which, being put, it passed in the negative."

Thus a full account has been given of this transaction, to which much importance has been attached by the committee of the Corporation in their report aforesaid of Nov., 1856; and your committee are persuaded that at said meeting of the Overseers, a majority of the members present, being satisfied that the movement had been got up by zealous and heated politicians, for the purpose of preventing Mr. Kneeland, or any other person, to whom they had objections, from holding the situation of steward, resolved for various reasons to defeat the project by the old parliamentary practice of moving the previous question, whereby the necessity of voting on the precise question raised might be avoided, and the whole matter would be indefinitely postponed. The previous question was therefore moved, and the vote being taken whether the main question should be then put, it was decided in the negative, and the whole subject was thus got rid of and postponed indefinitely.

The majority were unwilling to have the main question decided in the affirmative or the negative, and without doubt they believed that the worst thing that could happen would be to have it pass in the affirmative; for they understood that if such should be the result, the Corporation might not assent to it, and then a most unprofitable controversy would arise between the two Boards, with as much annoyance to one as the other; and if the Corporation should acquiesce in such a result, it would be necessary to change the practice, which, from the beginning, had worked so well, and all the members of the Board, after the heat engendered on that occasion had subsided, would regret the change, and be annoyed by having formal orders or votes laid before them for approval or disapproval, by which such a functionary as the steward had been elected; and probably a further movement would be made to have the rule extended to the selection or election of a baker, brewer, butler, cook, carpenter, and sweeper.

For these, and perhaps other reasons, the major part at said meeting, held in Dec., 1778, chose to have no change made respecting the steward, who, by the laws and usages of the college, was entitled to no recognition or mark of respect from the students, and was exposed to indignities and all kinds of rudeness from them on account of the peculiar services and various disagreeable duties he was obliged to perform, some of which were very offensive to the students, as the history of the college fully discloses.

The Overseers on this occasion, as at all times previously, preferred not to have any question acted upon, or agitated, as to their having any rights in relation to the employment or election of steward and the servants below him. The course pursued for more than two hundred years on this subject by the Corporation and the Overseers is deserving of special commendation. The Overseers have shown much practical wisdom touching all these inferior and smaller matters, by uniformly adhering to the observance of the sound and safe maxim, "*De minimis non curat lex.*"

In the judgment of your Committee the foregoing

practice, according to which the Corporation have chosen or employed the steward and all other servants below the grade of officers of instruction and government, without consulting the Overseers, or asking their approval, has no tendency, nor does it begin to have any tendency, to show that the Overseers do not possess the right of approval or disapproval in relation to the appointment of all officers of instruction and government, and any others that have been or may be raised above the grade of steward. No one will venture to say that there are not some persons engaged in the service of the college, whose employment by the Corporation it would be most absurd and ridiculous to present to the Overseers for their approval or disapproval. The line must be drawn somewhere, and whether the subject is considered in the legal point of view, founded on some claim of inherent power of the Corporation as aforesaid, or as a mere practical matter, it was without doubt appropriate, especially for a considerable time after the date of the charter, that the line of demarcation should be occupied by the steward; and the same having been adopted at such early period, under the circumstances then existing, it has been deemed proper not to change it since that time. The reasons for this course, and the actual necessity of the thing, were most obvious and conclusive.

On the other hand, your Committee insist, with the utmost confidence, that the universal practice on the part of the Corporation, to adopt a formal order or vote in every case where an officer of instruction and government, or other functionary partaking of that character, or raised to that dignity, was to be chosen, and to lay such order or vote before the Overseers for their approval or disapproval, is conclusive evidence that the Corporation have at all times believed that the Overseers possessed such right of approval or disapproval, and of course that they derived it from the charter and laws. Not only has such been the uniform and uninterrupted practice, but there never has been a suggestion or intimation of a doubt of such a right of approval or disapproval, till a doctrine adverse to such right was first broached in said report to the Corporation of Nov., 1856.

With regard to removals of officers of government and instruction, several instances have occurred since the date of the charter, some of which have been of an important character, and the practice has been the same as in the case of appointments of such officers. On no occasion has the removal of an instructor or officer of government been made without the action or approval of the Overseers. All orders or votes, by which *orders and by-laws* have been made by the Corporation, have at all times been laid by them before the Overseers for their concurrence.

Your Committee regard this practice of the Corporation and Overseers respecting the making of appointments of officers of instruction and government, also of removals, and of orders and by-laws, as in full accordance with the first, third, and fourth parts or provisions of the third clause of the charter; and in their judgment this practice is a strong confirmation of the claim of the Overseers, that they possess the right of approval or disapproval touching said appointments and removals, as well as said orders and by-laws, and derive the same from said proviso to the third clause; and it goes far to prove that the Overseers have, by virtue of said proviso, the same right as to salaries, embraced in the second or remaining part or provision of the third clause.

The action of the two Boards under the second part or provision of the third clause, which relates to the making of allowances to the officers of instruction and government of the college, alone remains to be considered. The practice of the two Boards respecting this matter is by no means so intelligible and satisfactory as their practice with regard to appointments, removals, and *orders and by-laws*. What may have been the reason why such a different course of things as to allowances or salaries has existed, your Committee are unable fully to ascertain or explain.

With regard to the allowance made by the Corporation, without consulting the Overseers, to the steward and other servants below the rank of officers of instruction and government, there is no difficulty. It could not but be expected that the same practice would at all times be pursued; and such a practice has in fact been pursued, as to the allowances to the steward, and servants of the same grade or below him, as has existed from the beginning respecting the selection or employment of them. The reasons in both cases have been the same, and the Overseers have always acquiesced in the practice.

For the first seventy-one or seventy-two years after the date of the charter, it does not appear that any order or vote of the Corporation, by which the salary of any officer of instruction and government was established or allowed, was laid before the Overseers for their approval; and no complaint on the part of the Overseers of the omission seems to have been made;

and it is believed no reason is stated in the records or history of the college for this course of things.

It is proper to remark, however, that, during this period, the college was poor and in straitened circumstances (the whole annual "real revenue" of the college, applicable to its general purposes, in 1654, being twelve pounds), the number of instructors and officers was small, the allowances were necessarily very limited, and the means of payment were precarious. The chief solicitude at that time related to the procuring of the means to pay the small salaries of these instructors and officers, and the Board of Overseers would not be likely to trouble themselves about the orders or votes of the Corporation on this subject. It would seem that the chief reliance was upon subscriptions and contributions.

For a long period after the date of the charter, the President of the college depended for his moderate allowance mainly on special grants to him by the General Court, and for many years, as it has been stated by the committee of the Corporation in their report of Nov. 1856, grants were made by the General Court of moneys to be distributed between the President and Fellows according to the determination of the *Overseers* of the college. Donations were also made by the town of Portsmouth "to be improved by the *Overseers* of the college for the advancement of good literature there." Other donations were probably given in like manner. The Overseers, thus having the chief funds at their disposal, frequently made appropriations of allowances to Fellows, and others, without any action of the Corporation upon them. In September, 1670, the Corporation voted "to speak to" the Overseers for the enlarging of the butler's stipend.

In January, 1673, the Overseers voted to pay to Dr. Leonard Hoar £100 towards his transportation to this country. These votes show that, for a considerable period, the Overseers had funds under their control, which they appropriated according to their own discretion, alone, towards providing for the wants of the college; especially, in support of its instructors and officers. The institution was poor, and it required constant exertion on the part of both Boards and of the friends of the college to obtain the means for supplying its wants.

Under such circumstances, it often happened that one Board could obtain means of relief, and raise money in certain quarters, more successfully than the other; and it was found that in many cases the college would derive the most benefit from the separate and independent action of each Board. The Board of Overseers was, much of the time, composed of powerful and influential men, and their aid was invoked to raise money by their single efforts, in which way they could accomplish much more than by acting in formal concert with the other Board. The aid of the Overseers was sought on such occasions in the same manner as their influential interposition was solicited to take the *initiative* and go forward and try a certain professor for divers misdemeanors, and remove him from office, and also to deal with a powerful and unmanageable treasurer, who had been guilty of various derelictions of duty.

It seems that the Corporation spoke to the Overseers, and begged them to render some aid to this officer, and certain aid to that; and, without doubt, the Overseers spoke to the Corporation, and desired them to make a small allowance out of the pittance of funds in the hands of the college treasurer, promising that they would furnish a certain sum to make up the balance of the amount required. Thus the Corporation, by speaking to the Overseers, and the Overseers, by speaking to the Corporation, contrived to raise the means by which the college officers might be rescued from starvation. After the two Boards had thus consulted together, and the Overseers had promised to furnish a specified amount, and the Corporation had agreed to vote a certain sum towards the support of one of the college officers, would it be expected, or considered necessary, that the Corporation should lay before the Overseers, for their approval, a formal order or vote, by which the grant, previously agreed upon as aforesaid, had been made?

In this way matters went on down to the year 1685, after which time, although some of the great difficulties and causes of irregularity had been removed, and the Corporation granted allowances and salaries every year, yet the amounts were undoubtedly small, and as the Corporation had not previously, for the causes aforesaid, and perhaps for other reasons of which we are ignorant, asked the approval by the Overseers of their orders or votes respecting salaries, they went on in their old track down to the year 1722, and omitted, as on all former occasions, to lay their action before the Overseers, who — not having been accustomed to have their approval asked, and not being aware that any considerable change in the state of things had occurred, and in consequence, perhaps, of other circumstances, a knowledge of which has not come down to the present generation — did not deem the matter to be of sufficient importance to make any complaint about it.

In 1722 and 1723 votes of the Corporation, by which

a Hebrew Instructor was appointed, and a grant to him was made of a salary of eighty pounds, were passed, and sent to the Overseers for their concurrence, and were approved. About this period the question in relation to certain salaries was raised and discussed, it being insisted that the Overseers had the right of approval or disapproval of the orders or votes of the other Board establishing salaries, which right was denied by the Corporation.

This question was again agitated about the year 1732; but no recognition of the claim of the Overseers as to salaries was obtained from the Corporation, which Board continued to pass orders or votes establishing salaries and making allowances, which orders or votes they omitted to present to the Overseers for approval, till the seventh of September, 1761, on which day the Corporation adopted votes, by which they established for the then ensuing year the salaries for the officers of instruction and government, and for the treasurer and the clerk of the Overseers, and these were transmitted to the Overseers and laid before them at their meeting in the succeeding month of October.

From this time forward down to about the year 1811, a period of about fifty years, all the numerous orders or votes of the Corporation, establishing annually the salaries of the officers of instruction and government, or making special grants to them, were uniformly presented to the Overseers for approval, and were, in every instance, confirmed by the Board. On the 26th of November, 1810, the Corporation passed divers votes or orders, prescribing the salaries of the several officers of instruction and government in the college, and also the salary of the treasurer and that of the secretary of the Board of Overseers, with a provision, that all such salaries, so established, should continue to be the salaries of such instructors, officers, etc., to be paid to them quarter-yearly, until the same should be altered by the Corporation, *with the approbation of the Overseers.* The orders or votes, adopted by the Corporation, as aforesaid, on the 26th November, 1810, were laid before the Overseers, for their approval, on the sixth day of the month of December following.

After the year 1810 the Corporation omitted to present their orders or votes, by which salaries were established or altered, to the Overseers for their approval, as they had done every year for the fifty successive previous years.

The Rev. John Thornton Kirkland was inaugurated President of Harvard College in November, 1810; and one of the first acts under his administration was the adoption by the Corporation of the vote aforesaid, on the 26th of that month, by which it was provided that the salaries, granted to the officers of the college the previous year, should thenceforth be paid to them until the same should be altered by said Board with the approbation of the Overseers. By reason of this vote the practice of prescribing and adjusting the salaries was changed, and thus they were made to continue for an indefinite period, and to remain permanent. When this was done, the Corporation omitted to lay before the Overseers the orders or votes by which they increased, changed or prescribed any of the salaries, as they had done every year for the preceding fifty years. Of course the Overseers received no information from the Corporation, and had no knowledge of their acts and doings in relation to salaries or special grants to the officers of instruction and government of the college.

It is true that for several years past the Treasurer's Annual Report has every year been laid before the Overseers, in which the amounts paid during the year to the officers of the college for their respective salaries are stated; but the report contains no express notice of any particular changes which have been made of the salaries in the course of the financial year to which the report relates. Such has continued to be the course of things, touching salaries, to the present time.

Since the year 1810, there have been two important alterations by the General Court of the constitution of the Board of Overseers, by means of which the Board was made to consist of a very large proportion of new members. In the year 1855, the Board consisted of many new members under a recent new organization of the Board by the Legislature, and in the course of a discussion, at a meeting of the Overseers during that year, respecting the Plummer Professorship of Christian Morals, pointed reference was made to the subject of salaries. In consequence of what occurred on that occasion, a committee was appointed to consider the relative powers, duties, and responsibilities of the President and Fellows, and of the Overseers of Harvard College, more especially in relation to salaries, etc., etc. This committee made their report, in January, 1856, as stated at the commencement of this report, in which it was insisted that the Overseers had the right of approval or disapproval of the orders or votes of the Corporation, by which salaries were established, by virtue of the proviso to the third clause of the charter of Harvard College.

After said report was presented and accepted by this

Board, a committee, consisting of the same members as the former committee, was appointed to confer with a like committee on the part of the Corporation relating to the questions at issue between the two Boards. This last committee on the part of the Overseers had several conferences with said committee of the Corporation. At the first of these meetings, the committee of the Overseers read to the committee on the part of the Corporation the form of two resolutions, or joint rules, with the adoption of which alone, or any other, substantially accomplishing the same object, they stated they should be entirely satisfied and content.

These two joint rules, or resolutions, were as follows, viz: —

1st. It shall be the duty of the President of the university, in a reasonable time, to lay before the Board of Overseers for their approval all votes or resolves of the Corporation, by which any bequests or donations for the use of the college, made for the promotion of specific objects and purposes, or encumbered with special trusts and conditions, shall by said Corporation be accepted.

2d. It shall be the duty of the President, without any unnecessary delay, to present to the Overseers for their concurrence all votes or orders of the Corporation, by which the salaries of any instructors and officers of government in the college shall be established or modified, or by which any special grants shall be made to such instructors and officers.

These two committees failed to come to any adjustment touching the matters in controversy, and the committee of the Corporation made their report to their Board in November, 1856, as aforesaid, and the committee on the part of the Overseers made a report to their Board on the 20th of January, 1857, stating as concisely as possible (the chairman being then very ill) their endeavors to procure the adoption of said joint rules, with some remarks by way of explanation, and prayed to be discharged from the further consideration of the subject. The request of said committee was granted by the Board, and they were discharged accordingly.

At a meeting of the Overseers, held a short time subsequently, the Hon. Reuben A. Chapman, a member of the Board, offered the following resolve, viz : —

Resolved, That, in the opinion of this Board, the appointment of officers, fixing the salaries of officers, and the acceptance of all donations and bequests, which are accompanied by conditions or special trusts, are among the things which it is the duty of the Corporation to lay before this Board for our action thereon.

This resolve, being explained by the mover, and its adoption ably advocated by the Hon. E. Rockwood Hoar and Hon. Francis Bassett, was passed by the Overseers without a division. It is a source of much satisfaction to this Board that their rights were vindicated and supported on said occasion by two learned lawyers, who are now justices of the Supreme Judicial Court of the Commonwealth.

Thus it appears that during this whole history in relation to salaries, the Corporation has for about three quarters of the time, since the date of the charter, omitted to lay their orders or votes, prescribing salaries, before the Overseers for approval. Of this the Overseers made no complaint for the first seventy-one or seventy-two years, but since that period they have on divers occasions complained of the omission, and insisted that they had the right of approval or disapproval of the doings of the Corporation respecting salaries, secured to them by the charter.

The right of the Overseers cannot be regarded as in any degree impaired by the lapse of time, during which such omission has been continued, especially when it is considered that the Overseers have not failed, on divers times, seriously to insist upon their claim, and that the President and Fellows have occasionally laid their orders or votes on this subject before the Overseers; and this the Corporation once did as to the salaries of officers of instruction and government and of the Treasurer every year during a period of fifty successive years. Although the Overseers have sometimes, for a considerable period, submitted in silence to the omission of the Corporation to comply with what the Overseers have regarded as an express and clear provision of the charter, yet in no case have they ever, when the question has been brought forward or agitated, hesitated to claim their right by the charter of approval or disapproval as to the orders or votes of the Corporation respecting the salaries of officers of instruction and government.

In the report of November, 1856, of the Committee of the Corporation, they seem disposed to draw large conclusions from the silence of the Overseers on two or three occasions, the most important of which they state as follows, viz.: " The statutes and laws of the university underwent an entire revision by both Boards in the year 1848, and a code was adopted by their concurrence, after amendments by the Overseers. This code purports to contain all the laws of the university, including those of its general organization and government." The said committee say that "they look in vain for any article or suggestion, indicating that the action of the Corporation upon salaries or any financial matters is to be submitted to the Overseers, or be in any manner subject to their confirmation or revision;" and they add that "it is submitted with great confidence that clearer proof could not be exhibited, that, up to the time of the revision and establishment of that code, in 1848, the Overseers did not claim, and did not imagine that they possessed the power of revising and controlling the action of the Corporation . . . in the establishment of salaries."

Your Committee agree with said committee of the Corporation that the object of both Boards in 1848 was to prepare a code which should contain all the laws of the university, including those of its general organization and government. The design evidently was to declare what should thenceforth be considered, not only the orders and by-laws of the university, but also to promulgate, in suitable, clear and convenient phraseology, those provisions of the charter and of the laws supplementary thereto, with regard to which said Boards are most frequently called upon to take action; and, without doubt, it was intended to set forth these provisions in such a form as should present the construction that had uniformly been given to them with the uninterrupted acquiescence of both Boards.

Of course, when the two Boards came to a provision of the charter, about the meaning or construction of which they could not agree, an enunciation of the meaning or legal effect thereof was necessarily omitted. It is very probable that the two Boards would on this, as they had on several former occasions, disagree when they came to that part of the charter which relates to the establishment of salaries.

This therefore is a good reason why no declaration was made on the subject of the salaries of officers of instruction and government, and the omission is no more adverse to the construction which the Overseers have put upon the provision in the third clause of the charter touching salaries, than it is to that which the Corporation has claimed.

It also should be particularly remembered that the Corporation, having in this case, as in all others, the initiative, prepared this new edition and digest of the laws, adopted it by a formal vote, and then laid the same before the Overseers, who concurred therein, with the exception of one unimportant paragraph, which was indefinitely postponed. The whole of the existing digest and edition of the laws, published in 1848, was the original work of the Corporation, and the question may well be asked why they omitted any declaration as to their powers respecting salaries. Two reasons only can be given. One is that they knew they had not an exclusive power over the subject (which fact, however, they might not be willing to acknowledge). The other is that they well understood, if they should make a declaration, asserting such exclusive power on their part, that the Overseers would not concur in any such declaration.

It is difficult to conceive how the Overseers can be considered as prejudiced by this omission on the part of the Corporation. When this code was laid before the Overseers, they might well have said that, although they should have been pleased to have had the Corporation insert a declaration that they had the power to establish salaries, subject to the approval or disapproval of the Overseers, yet, as the Corporation had altogether omitted the subject of salaries, a non-concurrence by the Overseers in the adoption of the said code or digest would be likely to lead to a defeat or loss of the whole work. Therefore the Overseers voted to concur. They perceived that such action on their part could never be regarded as an admission adverse to their right of approval or disapproval respecting salaries, but, on the contrary, the omission by the Corporation to insert a declaration that they possessed the exclusive power as to the establishment or modification of salaries was a circumstance significant and adverse to their possessing any such power.

Again, as the committee of the Corporation have undertaken to draw an inference adverse to the rights of the Overseers from the omission of any reference, in said edition of 1848 of the laws, to the subject of salaries, your Committee think proper to allude to certain things that are not only not passed over in silence, but fully expressed therein. One matter they will refer to, which they deem of much significance and importance. It is contained in article twenty-eight, which is in these words: "All the officers of instruction and government in the university are chosen by the Corporation with the concurrence of the Overseers, and are subject to removal for inadequate performance or neglect of duty or misconduct."

Here are substantially set forth in plain modern phraseology two of the provisions of the third clause in the charter, under which the Corporation make appointments and removals, subject to the concurrence of the Overseers. This is a simple and distinct assertion that the Corporation make appointments and removals of officers of instruction and government, and that the Overseers exercise the right of approval or disapproval thereof. This is a declaration of the construction of said two provisions in said third clause, which the Corporation and Overseers have adopted and acted upon from the first moment of the charter, for a period of more than two hundred years. Must not a construction, adopted and acted upon for such a length of time with perfect uniformity and unanimity, without the suggestion of a doubt, and in 1848 stated and confirmed in a new and authentic edition of the laws, affecting the college and sanctioned by both Boards, be regarded as the true construction, which must govern and prevail in all cases of future action on the part of either Board, or of intercourse between the Corporation and Overseers? As then the Corporation must be considered as having made these appointments and removals of officers of instruction and government for this long period by virtue of the said third clause, and laid their orders or votes on the subject before the Overseers for their approval, and as the Overseers have during all this time exercised this right of approval or disapproval, must they not be regarded as exercising it under the clause of the charter by which the Corporation made the said appointments and removals, that is, by virtue of the proviso to said clause ?

In the course of these two hundred years and upwards there must have been certainly several, and probably many, appointments and some removals, about which much division of sentiment must have prevailed, and great and perhaps intense excitement has existed.

Is it possible, then, if there had been any doubt as to the right of approval or disapproval by the Overseers of the orders or votes by which the Corporation made such appointments or removals, that the Corporation should never in a single instance have withheld the order or vote by which they made an appointment or removal, and omitted to lay it before the Overseers?

Your Committee believe they may with perfect confidence say that the Overseers have never on any occasion expressly or impliedly admitted that they did not, by virtue of said proviso, possess the right of approval or disapproval of the orders or votes adopted by the Corporation in relation to appointments, removals or salaries of officers of instruction and government, unless they did so by virtue of a report, which a committee of that Board, appointed Nov. 20, 1760, made in the year 1761, and which the committee of the Corporation, in their report of Nov. 1856, have dwelt upon at some length with apparent satisfaction.

The facts respecting said matter are as follows, viz.: At a meeting of the Overseers, held on the 20th of Nov., 1760, they adopted the following vote, viz.: "*Voted*, That there be a committee to consider whether it is in the power of the Corporation to make allowances to those who are employed in the government or instruction of the college, without the consent of the Overseers," and a committee of five was then appointed. This committee afterwards, in 1761, made a report, which was read, and the 9th of July, 1761, was specially assigned for its consideration, and it was voted that the Corporation be served with a copy thereof. This report was not taken up for consideration at said adjourned meeting in July, nor was it alluded to. It does not appear that it was ever accepted by the Overseers, and no further notice was taken of it on their records, and no allusion was ever made to it on the records of the Corporation.

The question now is, what was the character and contents of said report? As it has been stated, this report is not set forth or recorded, in whole or in part, on the books of the Corporation or of the Overseers. The said committee of the President and Fellows in their report of November, 1856, have produced two documents, one of which they say is the report aforesaid, made to the Overseers in 1761, and the other they call the answer of the Corporation to the same. The paper called the report of the committee of the Overseers made in 1761, purports to be signed by "Andrew Oliver, per order," the first person named on the said committee appointed the 20th of November, 1760. In said supposed report it is stated that the committee had consulted the charter, and had come to the conclusion that the Corporation had no right to make allowance to persons employed in the government of the college without the consent of the Overseers, and that this right of approval as to salaries is claimed by virtue of the fifth clause of the charter. It is remarked also in said paper that "the officers intended in the third clause of the charter are neither the President nor Fellows, nor any concerned in the government of the college, *but such officers as are ranked after the scholars of the college;* the officers here intended, no doubt, are the steward and butler, and any other officers (if such there be) not concerned in the government of the college."

It is, in fact, substantially denied in said paper that the Corporation has by virtue of the third clause of the charter any authority to elect officers of instruction and government, but only such mere ministerial agents or servants as aforesaid, the choice of whom, as it is alleged, is in the Corporation, independent of the Overseers.

The committee of the Corporation, in their report of November, 1856, to that Board, repudiate the doctrine contained in said old paper, by which the power of the Corporation to elect officers of government and instruction under the third clause is virtually denied, but they seem to be well satisfied with the conclusion therein that the Overseers have no right of approval or disapproval as to appointments made by the Corporation under said clause. It is difficult to comprehend how a committee, whether able and learned, or of ordinary capacity, could have made such a poor and imperfect report, as is contained in said old document. All the important and essential powers of both Boards, granted by the provisions of the third clause, are disallowed and denied in the paper.

When allusion is made in said document to the third clause, it is a matter of regret that its provisions were not set forth, especially that the proviso to the clause was not stated in the very words thereof, so that it might be certain that no error had occurred, and that the meaning and force of said proviso were understood.

The question now is, whether said old paper, produced by the committee of the Corporation in their report of November, 1856, is *the* report which was actually made in 1761 by the committee of the Overseers, appointed November 20, 1760. There is no circumstance which satisfactorily proves its identity or authenticity. Every one, conversant with legislation and the files of our Senate or House of Representatives, knows that in a controverted case, especially where there has been a large committee, consisting of five, seven, or more members, they may be divided, and after a hearing, and long discussion amongst themselves, the committee assembles to make a decision and take a final vote, and decide upon a report to be submitted to the Senate or House. On such an occasion the chairman thinks it important for him to come to the meeting prepared with a report, signed by him for the committee, expecting and hoping that his views will meet the approbation of his associates; in addition to which there may be one or more additional reports drawn up and signed by one or more members.

It sometimes happens that in a question of difficulty and doubt, each member comes with a report, expressing views peculiarly his own. This might well be the case where the members of a committee had undertaken to make up their minds respecting the meaning of the several clauses, or the several parts of a clause, in such an instrument as the college charter, and that too without the benefit of having heard an argument from learned counsel.

Again, in searching amongst old files of twenty, thirty or fifty years previous, it frequently happens that in the case sought for not an original paper can be found, and great disappointment is not unfrequently experienced in finding other papers, for the most part of no consequence, but as to *the* important document sought for, it cannot be discovered. So, where there may have been several reports in a case, one or more may be found, but the real one, which was finally adopted by the committee and presented, is missing.

When several reports are made, they may be similar in some particulars, and very different in other respects. So here the real report may have contained no notice of the third clause of the charter, but may have dwelt on the fifth clause, while the chairman may have drawn up his views as expressed in the old paper produced, in which the third clause is particularly noticed.

The said committee of the Corporation, in their report of November, 1856, have particularly referred to another old paper, produced by them, which they say is an answer made by the President and Fellows to the said supposed report to the Overseers in 1761. This is a paper about which more doubt, if possible, exists as to its authenticity than as to said paper signed by Andrew Oliver. It is not signed by the President, or any committee of the Corporation. There is no trace of any action on the subject of such reply either on the records of the Corporation or of the Overseers.

When the question as to salaries was pending, in 1761, and a committee of the Overseers made a report, some one of the Corporation, or some ambitious professor or tutor, may have tried his hand at making a reply, and presented it to the President; but the same, never having been adopted or sent to the Overseers, found its way into some recess, and is now discovered amongst the relics of a century ago.

There is one thing in said supposed reply which deserves particular notice. It contains no reference to the third clause of the charter, which is somewhat enlarged upon in said paper purporting to be signed by Andrew Oliver. Now it can hardly be supposed that this passage in the supposed report of 1761 to the Overseers, which disparaged the powers conferred on the Corporation by said clause, would have been wholly passed over, without some slight notice at least, in the reply of the President and Fellows. This circumstance tends to show that the said paper, signed by Andrew Oliver, was not *the* report which the writer of the paper, called the reply, had before him.

For the reasons aforesaid your Committee cannot think that either of said two old papers are entitled to any consideration or confidence. It is quite certain that it would be very unsafe to draw any inference from either of them which would be prejudicial to the rights of the Overseers or the Corporation.

There is one circumstance, however, which, unexplained, your Committee are bound to admit has some significance. The paper, produced as the report of a committee of the Overseers, certainly expresses the opinion of one member of that Board, namely, that of Mr. Andrew Oliver, clearly opposed to the views taken by your Committee respecting the construction of the third clause of the charter, and if by possibility that paper is, contrary to the judgment of your Committee, the actual report made in 1761, then it must be confessed that it is an admission on the part of a majority of the committee present when the report was adopted, that the Overseers have not, by virtue of the proviso to the third clause of the charter, the right of approval or disapproval as to appointments, allowances, and removals, made by the Corporation.

It is to be regretted that Mr. Oliver did not state in his report the proviso to the third clause in the words thereof in full, by which it would have appeared what his reading was. A learned lawyer in the summer of 1855 remarked, in a conversation with the chairman of your Committee, that if the words of the proviso had been " the said *orders and by-laws,*" or some equivalent expression, it might have been difficult for the Overseers to claim, by virtue of said proviso, a right of approval or disapproval as to appointments, allowances and removals.

This remark made a decided impression on the mind of the chairman of your Committee; and when the paper aforesaid, signed by Andrew Oliver, was discovered, he felt much solicitude on the subject, and went immediately to Cambridge, and examined the original charter of Harvard College, and found that the word *orders* alone was contained in said proviso, that is, that no such word as *laws* or *by-laws* was associated with the word *orders* therein. The reading of the said proviso was found to be the same as that in the copy of the charter in the manual, which all the members of this Board are at the present day furnished with.

The present secretary of the Overseers having extensive and accurate knowledge with regard to all ancient matters connected with Harvard College, and the colony and province of Massachusetts Bay, it was supposed that he might be able to give some information on this subject. The chairman of your Committee therefore inquired of him whether he had ever seen any manual, which bore date, or appeared to have been published, or in use, at any time prior to the Revolution of 1776, and which contained a copy of the charter. To which question the secretary replied that he had never seen or heard of any such manual, containing a copy of the charter of the college.

At a subsequent period the chairman of your Committee called at the office of said secretary, and there spent some time in looking over several of the early volumes of the Overseers' records; and his attention was attracted to the fact that in two or three instances meetings of the Board were called, or held by adjournment, for the purpose of considering some question in relation to certain rights of the Overseers under the charter; and that on one or more occasions the secretary was instructed, inasmuch as the Board was not in possession of the charter, etc., to lay before said Board copies of the charter and appendix for their inspection, that they might be able to decide some point or matter pending before them.

The question then arose in the mind of the chairman of your Committee whether the copies of the charter, which on any occasion the secretary thus laid before the Overseers, or furnished to any member of the Board, were correct copies, and whether there were any means of ascertaining that fact, or of learning what the secretary made or derived his copies from, — whether from the original charter in the custody of the President at the college, or from some authenticated copy thereof. He then inquired of the secretary, who was present, how he supposed some one of the Overseers obtained a sight of the charter, or ascertained in the most convenient way what the provisions of the charter might be touching some particular matter, or from what source the secretary in former years had procured a copy thereof for the use of the Overseers, when he had been instructed to lay a copy before the Board.

"O," said the secretary, "a full copy of the charter and of the appendix is contained in the first volume of the records of the Overseers, where it was entered by tutor Flynt, secretary of the Board, and certified by him to be a true copy in each case. This was done about the year 1718. Whenever the Overseers, or any committee or member thereof, wished to see the charter or appendix, application was, without doubt, made to the secretary for an inspection thereof; and whenever the Overseers had any question before them, upon which some provision of the charter might be supposed to have a bearing, they would direct the secretary to lay a copy before them at the next meeting, and of course all he would have to do would be to put this first duodecimo volume in his pocket, and thus have at the meeting the charter and appendix, that is, authenticated copies thereof, for the inspection of the Overseers; and if some member of the Board should find any difficulty in reading the hand-writing of tutor Flynt, who made these copies, the tutor himself, or his successor, who had become familiar with the writing, would be ready to read and explain it."

As soon as the secretary explained in what way the Overseers in former days ascertained what were the contents of the charter, or what some particular provision of it might be, the chairman of your Committee at once desired the secretary to turn to the place in said first volume of the records where a copy of the charter as well as of the appendix was to be found, and point out the third clause of the charter, and especially the proviso at the end thereof. The important proviso was then pointed out, and behold it read as follows, viz.: "Provided the said *laws* and orders be allowed by the Overseers." Thus the perplexing mystery was revealed, and the great difficulty was explained. This perfectly accounted for the fog that beclouded the mind of Andrew Oliver, who wrote the old paper aforesaid of 1761.

Your Committee have thus travelled over much ground in the examination of the various questions that arise respecting the third clause of the college charter, and the proviso to the same. They will now present a sort of recapitulation, or rather restatement, of the positions they have endeavored to establish, and will add such other points and remarks as may, in their approach to the end of their report, occur to them.

1st. The first great and paramount object of the charter was to establish a corporation, in which the title to all the property belonging to the college, real and personal, might be vested, of which property the Corporation should in law have the sole and absolute management; and the President and Fellows at the beginning, and at all times since, have without doubt acted on the principle that they possessed an incidental and inherent power of using all the means requisite to enable them to exercise this sole management of said property, without being liable to be controlled or affected by any *legal* right of interference or action on the part of the Overseers.

2d. The third clause is that part of the charter from which the President and Fellows derive all their *express* power to make appointments and removals of officers and servants of the college, also allowances to them and orders and by-laws. This point is now admitted by both Boards, and no question can hereafter be raised on the subject.

3d. The question then arises whether the Overseers have the right of approval of all orders or votes which the Corporation may pass by virtue of the provisions of said clause, and if they have not this right as to the action of the Corporation in all cases under this clause, then the inquiry should be in what cases the Overseers have the right.

The Overseers do not ask to have or exercise any right of approval or disapproval of the action of the Corporation by which the steward, or other servants below him, are chosen or employed, and they prefer to have the old practice continued, which has existed uninterruptedly from the beginning with regard to such inferior agents or servants as are selected or employed with reference to the management of the college property, and the material interests and business matters which are incidental to said property, or have any relation thereto. The Overseers are entirely indifferent *whether* this practice is considered as having existed from the beginning, or as now existing, by reason of a claim on the part of the Corporation of an inherent and original power, incidental to their sole and exclusive management of said property; or *whether* it grew out of the *necessity* of the case, and for that reason, and as a great relief to the Overseers, it was always cheerfully assented to and acquiesced in by them.

The Overseers are also willing and desirous to have the practice continued, by which the Corporation have at all times, without asking the previous consent or subsequent approval of the Overseers, determined what should be the compensation of the steward, and of all the servants below him, for their services, for the same reason they have chosen or employed such agents and servants without consulting the Overseers, or desiring their approval.

4th. Whenever college appointments are mentioned or alluded to by some one educated at the university, or having any connection with it, or knowledge of its concerns, the appointments of the *officers of instruction and government* are alone intended; no reference whatever is had on such occasions to the steward, or to the servants below him.

The chief matter which the Overseers can feel any interest about, when appointments, salaries and removals are alluded to, relates to the appointments, salaries and removals of the officers of instruction and government, and the question is whether they have the right of approval or disapproval of the orders or votes by which the Corporation under the third clause make such appointments and removals, and establish salaries, as well as make orders and by-laws. It always has been and still is admitted by the President and Fellows that the Overseers have, by virtue of the proviso at the end of the third clause of the charter, the right of approval or disapproval of all votes by which the Corporation pass orders and by-laws under the fourth part or provision of said third clause. The Overseers insist that said proviso applies also to the other three parts or provisions of said third clause, and that they have the right of approval or disapproval as to appointments, salaries and removals of officers of instruction and government, by virtue of said proviso, as well as they have the right as to orders and by-laws. This depends on the question whether the word *orders* in said proviso means the same as *votes*, or whether it signifies the same as *orders* and *by-laws*.

5th. The word *orders* in the proviso to the third clause signifies the same as *votes*. This fact is perfectly apparent on a perusal of the records of the colonial legislature and of the whole colonial history of Massachusetts, and is proved by the practice in towns and corporations in Massachusetts, and is shown by an examination of the writings of our statesmen, legislators and scholars, and also of the records of the Corporation of Harvard College; and this proviso with the word *orders,* having the same construction and signification as *votes,* manifestly gives to the Overseers the right of approval or disapproval of all votes by which the Corporation make appointments and removals, and establish salaries of officers of instruction and government, as well as make orders and by-laws. In Worcester's Dictionary, under the definition of the word "*vote*," the following citation is made from the Hon. L. S. Cushing's MANUAL OF PARLIAMENTARY PRACTICE, a work of high authority, viz.: "The judgment, opinion, sense, or will of a deliberative assembly is expressed, according to the nature of the subject, either by a RESOLUTION, ORDER, or VOTE."

6th. The construction aforesaid, put upon the proviso to the third clause of the charter, is distinctly admitted and confirmed so far as regards appointments, as has been already stated, by the memorial of the President and Fellows to the legislature of Massachusetts in the year 1851, in which they say, "It" (the charter) "gave to them" (the Corporation) "the sole power of appointing all OFFICERS AND SERVANTS OF THE COLLEGE, and vested in them the exclusive right of enacting rules and laws for its government, and administering them, subject only to the approval or disapproval of such APPOINTMENTS, *rules and laws by the Overseers.*" This is a clear and conclusive declaration that the Overseers have the right of approval or disapproval of the appointments of officers and servants of the college, made by the Corporation under said third clause, and it follows with perfect certainty that the Overseers must have this right by virtue of the proviso to said clause, and if that proviso applies to appointments, it must necessarily and inevitably apply to *salaries* and *removals*.

This is further confirmed not only as to *appointments*, but as to *removals*, by the joint action of the Corporation and Overseers which occurred in 1848. In a collection or new edition of the laws concerning the college, revised and approved by both Boards, there is set forth substantially, in article twenty-eight, the first and third provisions of the third clause of the charter, and also the proviso to said clause, as understood by your Committee; that is, the practical construction put upon the same by the Corporation and Overseers from the beginning, during a period of more than two hundred years, is declared in the following words, namely: — "All the officers of instruction and government in the university are chosen by the Corporation, with the concurrence of the Overseers, and are subject to removal for inadequate performance and neglect of duty or misconduct."

7th. It should be constantly recollected that the important admissions and declarations aforesaid of the Corporation that the Overseers possess the right of approval or disapproval as to appointments as in the said memorial of 1851, and as to appointments and removals of officers of instruction and government as in the code or edition of 1848 of the laws, were made on occasions favorable for accuracy of statement, and such admissions and declarations, made under such circumstances, have much more weight than an assertion of a claim by the Corporation, or by a committee of that Board, made in 1856, in the heat of a controversy, when a question was pending concerning such claim between the two Boards. It should also be remembered that *four* of the persons, who were members of the Corporation in 1848, when the said new edition and digest of the laws was prepared and adopted by that body, were members in 1851, when said memorial was presented to the House of Representatives, and were also members when said report of November 1856 was presented to and accepted by said Board, of which Board said *four* constituted a majority.

8th. Again, if the Overseers have the right of approval or disapproval as to appointments, as it is admitted by the Corporation in their said memorial of 1851, and if they have the same right as to appointments and removals as it is admitted and declared by the Corporation and Overseers in the edition of 1848 of the laws respecting the college, where would be the most obvious and natural place for the recognition of such a right of approval or disapproval? Would it not be where this proviso is? There is the appropriate, and in fact the necessary place for it, and it *must* be there, unless the language of this proviso forbids it.

Here is a proviso, at the end of the third clause, in which *some* right of approval or disapproval is given to the Overseers, and it always has been, and is now admitted by the Corporation that this proviso is applicable to one at least of the four parts or provisions of the third clause of the charter; and the reasons why it should be considered as applicable to each of the other three parts or provisions, are stronger and more exacting than any reason can be given for the applicability of said proviso to the last part or provision of said clause. The applicability of said proviso to all the four parts or provisions of said clause depends upon the meaning of the important word *orders* contained in said proviso. In order to confine the application to the fourth part or provision only of said third clause, this word *orders* must be made to signify the same as rules and regulations, or laws or by-laws, or orders and by-laws. The reasons are so strong however against the adoption of this signification of the word orders, and of a consequent narrow, partial, and wholly imperfect application and use of said proviso, that this word surely ought not to be so interpreted, provided it is capable of any other meaning.

Your Committee have demonstrated, as they believe, that this word, when standing alone, does not signify rules and regulations, or laws or by-laws, or orders and by-laws, but always, or almost always, it means the same as *votes*. Why then should not this be promptly and at once adopted as the true meaning of the word, by means whereof this important proviso is made applicable to all said parts or provisions of said third clause, including the first three as well as the fourth? When this question is placed in the scale of reason, common sense and clear evidence, the construction given to this word as bearing a meaning very similar to, or identical with, that of *votes*, preponderates with decisive and unremitting energy.

9th. When a professorship, or other new office in the college, is established, the matter is always submitted to the Overseers, and their concurrence is asked by the Corporation. On all such occasions, the question as to what shall be the salary of the incumbent of such new office of instruction or government, is an important element in the consideration of the Overseers. This also is the case at all times when appointments are made or approved. Appointments and salaries have important mutual relations. Action can hardly be taken by the

Overseers in relation to an appointment without reference to the salary of the appointee. If the Corporation in their order or vote, establishing a professorship or assistant professorship, prescribe the salary of the professor, and lay their doings before the Overseers, and the same are approved, the Corporation are under peculiar obligations, in addition to those imposed by the requirements of the charter, if they shall afterwards increase or change said salary, to ask the consent and approval of the Overseers. It is a violation of the understanding and substantial agreement between the two Boards, if the Corporation presume to increase, or otherwise change, the salary of an incumbent of such a new professorship, which salary was an important and essential part of the *transaction* when such professorship was established.

10th. Whether salaries should be established for an indefinite term, or for the specific term of one year only, will be a subject for the special consideration of the Corporation. As they have the initiative, they will of course have the matter under their entire control in this respect, and will adopt orders or votes, by which the salaries of the college officers and instructors shall be established for an indefinite period, or for the definite term of the then ensuing financial year.

11th. With regard to any apprehension on the part of the Corporation that the exercise by the Overseers of the right of approval or disapproval as to salaries might be a source of evil, or annoyance, your Committee are very confident that there is not the slightest ground for any such fear or anxiety. Every one, who has been for a considerable period an Overseer, well knows that it rarely happens there is a single member of the Board, who has not reasons for desiring the good will and favorable regard of the President of Harvard University. The Overseers must at all times understand and feel that the Corporation have the best means of knowing what the salaries of the officers of instruction and government ought to be, and they will always be disposed to approve the action of the Corporation touching salaries, unless on examining a particular case they shall be well satisfied that the doings of the Corporation are clearly wrong and ought to be corrected. The prevailing disposition of this Board will be to approve the votes of the Corporation respecting salaries, unless they receive an intimation from some member of the Corporation, or other person connected with the college, who is known to be desirous of promoting its best interests, that a special examination of one or more certain salaries should be made; and if any one of the Overseers should happen to be somewhat pragmatical, and should on some occasion object without good reason to the amount of a particular salary, the President and treasurer, being members of the Corporation, and ex-officio members of the Board of Overseers, will be present, and by their statements and explanations will very easily prevent any objectionable action on the part of this Board.

When the Corporation have on their minds the fact, that their doings are to be submitted to, and passed upon, by another Board, they will do their best to adjust the salaries in a reasonable, impartial and proper manner, so as to avoid all danger of a disapproval by such other Board of their order or vote, by which any salary may be established or modified. The best evidence as to this matter may be found in the history of the adjustment of salaries by the Corporation every year from 1761 to 1811. The Corporation took such good care to guard against partiality and favoritism, and in so judicious a manner to fix and regulate every year the salaries of the officers of instruction and government and of the treasurer, that not a word of objection or dissent was heard from the Overseers in a single instance, for these fifty successive years, which elapsed during a part of the administration of President Holyoke, the whole of the period during which Presidents Locke, Langdon, Willard, and Webber were in office, and the early part of the presidency of Dr. Kirkland.

12th. It is of great importance to the President and Fellows, and also to the college, that they should at all times comply with the provisions of the charter. Is it not their duty and a matter of high expediency to refrain from any action which may be considered as a disregard of the just rights of the Overseers? Would it not be much better for the Corporation to abstain from exercising their own full rights than to exceed their powers in a single instance, and if a question arises whether they should lay their orders or votes before the Overseers touching a certain subject for approval, will it not be the wisest course for them to act in accordance with the wishes of the lower Board, when a contrary action would be attended with much doubt, and the adoption of the course desired by the Overseers can never be a source of any injury or danger to the college, or a matter of any annoyance or inconvenience to the Corporation, but manifestly may be beneficial to the university and satisfactory to the great body of its able and judicious friends?

Again, if at any time a radical movement against the

Corporation should be conceived, the projectors will never fail to avail themselves of some violation or disregard of the charter by that body as their chief ground of assault, if such a violation or disregard has actually occurred, and is known to such projectors, or if a case of such violation can be made out with a tolerable show of argument. If in 1851 the circumstance of the omission by the Corporation for several previous years to lay their orders or votes respecting salaries before the Overseers for approval had been known, and fully understood, as it has been since, the bill then introduced for remodelling the Corporation might have passed. It should always be remembered that the Board of Overseers consists of the Governor and Lt. Governor of the State, the President of the Senate, the Speaker of the House, and the Secretary of the Board of Education, and thirty other gentlemen, *chosen by the legislature*, and a part of them are chosen every year.

It is believed that there are not now, and there have not been for a long time, any real matters of disagreement between the two Boards, except such as relate to salaries, and to bequests or donations, made for the promotion of specific objects and purposes, or accompanied with special trusts and conditions. Let the Corporation, then, hereafter lay all their orders or votes before the Overseers for their concurrence, by which salaries of officers of instruction and government shall be established or modified, or special allowances shall be made to them, or by which the bequests or donations above specified shall by said Corporation be accepted. By this course the President and Fellows will guard their body and the university against assault or danger, will give entire satisfaction to the Overseers, remove all grounds of complaint, do much good to the college, and in no way subject themselves to any inconvenience or annoyance.

The result will be that perfect harmony and mutual confidence will exist between the two Boards, and their united power will be sure to be available in the most effective way to oppose and resist all assaults on the college, or on either of said Boards, from whatever quarter they may come.

13th. The attention of your Committee has just been called to the following important passage in Mr. Quincy's History of the university, viz.: —

"On the 4th of January, 1821" (in the convention for revising the constitution of Massachusetts), "the Hon. Daniel Webster as chairman of a committee made a report to the convention, in which, after a short recapitulation of important points in the history of the college, they declare their opinion concerning the existing constitution of that seminary, — that it is a well-contrived and useful form of government. The Corporation consists of but few persons; they can, therefore, assemble frequently and with facility, for the transaction of business, either regular or occasional. The Board of Overseers, having a negative on the MORE IMPORTANT ACTS OF THE CORPORATION, is a large and popular body, a great majority of its members being such as are annually elected to places in the highest trust in the government by the people themselves. A MORE EFFECTUAL CONTROL OVER THE PROCEEDINGS OF THE CORPORATION CANNOT BE DESIRED. Indeed, if a new government were now to be framed for a university, independent of all considerations of existing rights and privileges, the committee do not know that a better system could probably be devised."

This committee consisted of the Hon. Daniel Webster, Hon. Samuel S. Wilde, Hon. Samuel Dana, Hon. H. A. S. Dearborn, and Allen Tillinghast, Esq. In their report, made to the constitutional convention of 1820, it is declared that "the OVERSEERS HAVE A NEGATIVE ON THE MORE IMPORTANT ACTS of the Corporation," and that "A MORE EFFECTUAL CONTROL OVER THE PROCEEDINGS OF THE CORPORATION CANNOT BE DESIRED." Now the appointing of officers of instruction and government in the college, the establishing of their salaries, and the removal of such functionaries from office by the Corporation in pursuance of the provisions of the third clause of the charter, must certainly be considered as amongst "the MORE IMPORTANT ACTS OF THE CORPORATION." They are in fact acts of the very highest importance.

This opinion, declared concerning the charter and constitution of the college by two such learned and discriminating lawyers as Mr. Webster and Mr. Justice Wilde, in concurrence with other able and distinguished men on the committee, is entitled to the highest possible respect and confidence, and must be regarded as decisive in relation to the questions considered in this report, and as settling the same in accordance with the judgment and conclusions expressed by your Committee.

The chairman of your Committee having adopted the opinion of the late Hon. Samuel Hoar, his associate on a former committee, that the full and entire right of approval or disapproval as to appointments, salaries, removals and orders and by-laws, was secured to the Board of Overseers by the proviso to the third clause, and that there was no necessity whatever of resorting to any other part of the charter, or to the appendix, for such right, expressed to his colleagues on the committee at an early day his desire to rest on that proviso alone. The chairman assigned as reasons for this course, *first*, because that proviso gave to the Overseers full power in the premises, and, *secondly*, because of the understanding he had with Mr. Hoar not to have recourse to the appendix of the college charter, and he did not, after the decease of his excellent friend, feel at liberty to pursue a different course from that which he adopted in concert with him in his lifetime.

The other two members of the Committee, while concurring with the chairman in the opinion that the proviso to the third clause is ample for the purpose of conferring on the Overseers the right of approval or disapproval as aforesaid, reserve to themselves the right to insist, if they think proper, in any discussion that may be had, that the same right of approval or disapproval or revision by the Overseers is conferred or confirmed by the fifth clause of the charter or by the second clause of the appendix.

Your Committee will now proceed to state that by virtue of the instructions of the Board, contained in the order by which they were appointed, they have procured an accurate and perfect copy of the original charter of Harvard College, which copy, hereto annexed, they present to the Overseers, and they have compared the same with what purports to be a copy of said charter, which is entered in the first volume of the "separate records" of the Overseers, and certified to be a true copy by Henry Flynt, secretary; and the Committee find an important discrepancy between said true copy of the original, just procured as aforesaid, and said copy contained in the records of the Overseers, viz., the insertion of the two words "laws and" in said copy contained in the Overseers' records, which are not found in the original charter.

These two words are inserted in the proviso to the third clause of the charter, by means of which this proviso in said copy contained in the Overseers' records reads as follows, viz.: " provided the said *laws and orders* be allowed by the Overseers," instead of being in the words of the original charter, viz.: " provided the said ORDERS be *allowed* by the Overseers."

Your Committee have extended their report very far beyond the limits they at first expected or intended. They are aware that they may be charged with prolixity and repetition. But they have preferred to be too long rather than too short, to use more words than were necessary rather than too few, and they have chosen to indulge in repetition rather than to incur any danger of having some statement fail of being fully understood at the moment by reason of the reader's not finding with facility, what had been stated in some former part of the report. Your Committee have not studied order. They have stated facts and suggestions as they occurred to them, and have not undertaken afterwards to reduce the same to a more orderly arrangement. Such as it is, they present their report to the Board, with the hope that it will enable them to understand and determine the true meaning and construction of an important portion of the college charter. Your Committee conclude with recommending the adoption of the subjoined order.

All which is respectfully submitted.

GEORGE MOREY,
J. G. ABBOTT,
J. M. MANNING.

APPENDIX.

Acts and doings of the "Governors of Harvard College" prior to the date of the charter of 1650, *and of "the Corporation" afterwards, viz.:* —

"At the meeting of the Governors of Harvard College held in the college-hall this 27th of 10th, 1643."

"It is *ordered that* —

"1. The accounts of Mr. Harvard's gift are to be finished, and Mr. Pelham, Mr. Nowell, Mr. Hibbins, Mr. Syms, Mr. Wilson, are chosen to finish it, &c. &c.

"2. Mr. Pelham is elected Treasurer of the college by the joint vote of the Governors of the college."

"It *is ordered* that two Bachelors shall be chosen for the help of the President to read to the Junior pupils, as the President shall see fit, and be allowed out of the college Treasury 4£ per annum to each of them for their pains."

JUNE 17, 1667.

Ordered by *the Corporation*, that the Bachelors shall have the forenoon on the commencement day for the performance of their work, and that for the future it shall be looked upon as their due ordinarily, except there do appear to the President and Fellows any just reason, moving them to order it otherwise.

OCTOBER 4, 1669.

Ordered by *the Corporation*, that Mr. Thomas Danforth be desired, and upon his consent engaged, to pay unto the Fellows the money due by Charlestown Ferry, &c.

It *is also ordered* that three pounds be allowed by the steward to Goodman Taylor towards the discharge of the charges of his son's commencement; and that this money be repaid, either by the money coming from the eastward (if it be allowable), or to be allowed out of Mr. Webb's gift, abating fifteen shillings apiece, from the money aforesaid, distributed among four persons.

It is *further ordered* that the revenues of Mr. Webb's gift be distributed for the following year as it was the last year, viz. : that there be allowed to Sir Shephard four pounds; to Higginson three pounds; to Corlett three pounds; to Adams three pounds, and this money is to be allowed to them by the steward, unless some part thereof be *abated*, as is provided in the foregoing *order*.

Item — It is *ordered* that Sewall be made a scholar of the House; and succeed Sir Epes (provided that he leave the college in the winter) in his scholarship.

February 12, 1671.

Ordered by the *Corporation* that Sir Thatcher and Alcocke continue scholars of the House; and that Pyke and Allen be substituted in the other two vacant places.

Item — That the three pounds of Mr. Webb's gift, allowed to Sir Corlett for the year current, be given to Hawley, and that only one quarter's pay be allowed to Sir Corlett by reason of his discontinuance.

At a Corporation Meeting, May 27, 1673.

Mr. Thomas Graves being spoken with concerning his coming to be employed as fellow of the college, freely declared to the Corporation that he (upon consideration of the passed) was not free to accept any such employment.

Ordered, That Na. Gookin be declared successor unto Jere. Shephard, for the enjoying four pounds per annum of Mr. Webb's gift from the time of Mr. Shephard's leaving it, and during the pleasure of the Corporation.

March 1, 1674.

Ordered by *the Corporation* that Sir Sewall be from henceforth the keeper of the college Library.

April 15, 1674.

Ordered, That Mr. Gookin and Sir Sewall, fellows of the college, have half a year's salary of their proportion paid them of the Piscataway gift, now in the Treasurer's hands, according as the Honorable Overseers have directed the same to be proportioned.

At a Meeting of the Corporation, January 1, 1675.

Ordered, That Minot, Allen, Cheever, Danforth be scholars of the

House for the year ensuing; and that Allen receive five pounds due of the scholarship and to be presently paid.

AT A MEETING OF THE CORPORATION AT CAMBRIDGE, SEPT. 2, 1675.

Ordered by *the Corporation*, That Thomas Cheever shall be monitor.

DECEMBER 22, 1675.

Ordered by the Corporation, That Wadsworth be scholar of the House.

MARCH 22, 1682–3.

Ordered, That Eliot, Whiting, Mills, Phillips shall have each of them for the next year 5 pounds given to them out of the college revenue. This VOTE to begin from the 26th of this instant March.

DECEMBER 5, 1683.

Voted, That Walton be chosen Butler.

Ordered, That the scholars of the house for the year ensuing shall be Sir Mitchell, Sir Danforth, Dennison, Saltonstall, Dudley and Cotton.

Ordered, That upon consideration of the great pains, which the present fellows resident in the college, viz. Mr. Andrew and Mr. Cotton, have taken, their allowances for the year past, beginning at the commencement, 1682, shall be 45 pounds in money to each of them, and that what the income from the Ferry at Charlestown and Mr. Glover's gift does come short of this sum, shall be made up out of the money received in England by the Hon. Treasurer of the college, Major Richards.

AT A MEETING OF THE CORPORATION IN CAMBRIDGE, MARCH 17, 1683–4.

Voted, That Eliot, Whiting, Mills and Philips shall have each of them five pounds in money given to them.

This VOTE to begin from the 26th of March, 1684.

APRIL 20, 1691.

It *is ordered*, That the resident Fellows, viz. Mr. John Leverett and Mr. William Brattle, be allowed as their salary for this present year, five and twenty pounds each, besides what they have received, and what they are yet to receive from Charlestown Ferry.

AT A CORPORATION MEETING AT HARVARD COLLEGE, AUG. 6, 1694.

Ordered, 1st, That Sir Flint, Willard, Smith, Moody and Willard, Junior, be scholars of the House for this present year.

2d. That Mr. Pemberton be library keeper this year, and his allowance five pounds.

3d. That the salary of the resident Fellows be for the present year 50 pounds between them, to be paid by the Treasurer, besides what they shall receive from Charlestown Ferry.

MARCH 4, 1694–5.

Ordered, That the Treasurer pay unto the Rev. President or his order, what was ordered unto him of the interest money due from Mr. Edward Pelham anno 1686.

THE CHARTER OF HARVARD COLLEGE.

WHEREAS THROUGH THE good hand of God many well deuoted persons haue beene and dayly are mooued and stirred vp to giue and bestowe sundry guiftes legacies land^s and Revennewes for the aduancement of all good literature artes and Sciences in Haruard Colledge in Cambridge in the County of Middlesex and to the maintenance of the Præsident and ffellowes and for all accommodacŏns of Building^s and all other necessary prouisions that may conduce to the education of the English & Indian Youth of this Country in knowledge and godlines. IT IS therefore ordered and enacted by this Court and the aucthority thereof That for the furthering of so good a worke and for the purposes aforesaid from henceforth that the said Colledge in Cambridge in Middlesex in New England shalbe a Corporation Consisting of seauen persons (to wit) a President ffiue ffellowes and a Treasurer or Burser and that Henry Dunster shall be the first President Samuell Mather Samuell Danford maisters of Arte Jonathan Michell Comfort Starre and Samuell Eaton Batchelers of Arte shall be the fiue ffellowes and Thomas Danford to be present Treasurer, all of them being Inhabitant^s in the Bay, and shall be the first seuen persons of which the said Corporation shall consist And that the said seuen persons or the greater number of them procuring the presence of the Ouer-

seers of of the Colledge and by their counsell and
consent shall haue power and are heereby authorised
at any tyme or tymes to elect a new President ffellowes or Treasurer so oft and from tyme to tyme as
any of the said person or persons shall dye or be remoued. Which said President and ffellowes for the tyme
being shall for euer heereafter in name and fact be one
body politique and Corporate in Lawe to all intent^s
and purposes, and shall haue perpetuall succession And
shall be called by the name of President and ffellowes of
Haruard Colledge And shall from tyme to tyme be
eligible as afforesaid And by that name they and their
successors shall and may purchase and acquire to
themselues or take and receaue vppon ffree guift and
donation any Land^s Tenement^s or Hereditament^s
within this Jurisdicc͠on of the Massatusett^s not exceeding the value of ffiue hundred pound^s per annum
and any good^s and sommes of money whatsoeuer to
the vse and behoofe of the said President ffellowes and
Schollers of the said Colledge and also may sue and
plead or be sued and impleaded by the name aforesaid
in all Courtes and places of Judicature within the
Jurisdicc͠on aforesaid and that the said President with
any three of the ffellowes shall haue power and are
heereby Aucthorized when they shall thinck fitt to
make and appoint a Common Seale for the vse of the
said Corporation. And the President & ffellowes or
the maior part of them from tyme to tyme may meete
and choose such Officers & Servant^s for the Colledge
and make such allowance to them and them alsoe
to remoue and after death or remoueall to choose such
others and to make from tyme to tyme such orders
& Bylawes for the better ordering & carying on

the worke of the Colledge as they shall thinck fitt, Prouided the said orders be allowed by the Ouerseers. And also that the President and ffellowes or maior parte of them with the Treasurer shall haue power to make conclusiue bargaines for Landes & Tenement^s to be purchased by the said Corporation for valuable consideracõ. AND for the better ordering of the Gouerment of the said Colledge and Corporation Be it Enacted by the Aucthoritie aforesaid That the President and three more of the ffellowes shall and may from tyme to tyme vppon due warnīge or notice giuen by the President to the rest holde a meeting for the debating and concluding of affaires concerning the proffitt^s and Reuennues of any Landes, and disposing of their Good^s. Prouided that all the said disposing^s be according to the will of the Donors. And for direction in all emergent occasions execution of all orders and Bylawes and for the procuring of a Generall meeting of all the Ouerseers & societie in great & difficult cases, and in cases of nonagreement, In all which cases aforesaid the conclusion shall be made by the maior parte ye said President hauing a casting voice the Overseers consenting therevnto, And that all the aforesaid transaccõns shall tend to & for the vse and behoofe of the President ffellowes Schollers & Officers of the said Colledge and for all accomodacõns of building^s bookes and all other necessary prouisions & furnitures as may be for the aduancement & education of youth in all manner of good literatûre Artes and Sciences. AND further be it ordered by this Court and the Aucthority thereof That all the Landes Tenement^s or hereditament^s howses or Revennues within this Jurisdiccon. to the aforesaid President or Colledge appertayning not exceeding the value of fiue hundred pound[s] per annum shall from henceforth be freed from all ciuill impositions taxes & rates all good[s] to the said corporation or to any Schollers thereof appertayning shall be exempt from all manner of tolle Customes & excise whatsoeuer. And that the said President ffellowes & Schollers together with the servant[s] & other necessarie Officers to the said President or College appertayning not exceeding tenne, viz three to the President and seuen to the Colledge belonging shall be exempted from all personall ciuill offices militarie exercises or seruices watching[s] and warding[s]. and such of their estates not exceeding one hundred poundes a man shall be free from all Country taxes or rates whatsoeuer and none others. IN WITNES whereof The Court hath caused the Seale of the Colonie to be heerevnto affixed. Dated the One & thirtieth day of the Third moneth called May, Anno 1650.

IN BOARD OF OVERSEERS OF HARVARD COLLEGE,
February 20, 1862.

Ordered, That the secretary of the Overseers be instructed and directed to cause the correct and perfect copy of the charter of Harvard College, this day laid before this Board by their committee, to be inserted in the records of the Overseers; and that said secretary be also instructed to make in the margin of the page in the present record of what purports to be a copy of the charter in the first volume of the Overseers' records, a reference to the volume and page where said correct and perfect copy of the charter shall be inserted; and said committee are charged with the duty of seeing that the requirements of this order are fully complied with.

www.ingramcontent.com/pod-product-compliance
Lightning Source LLC
Chambersburg PA
CBHW020300090426
42735CB00009B/1161